The Smithsonian Treasury
THE PRESIDENTS

The Smithsonian Treasury

THE PRESIDENTS

Frederick S. Voss
NATIONAL PORTRAIT GALLERY

SMITHSONIAN INSTITUTION PRESS · WASHINGTON, D.C.

Title pages: View of Washington, D.C. from the Capitol, c. 1860.

Produced in cooperation with the Book Development Division, Smithsonian Institution Press.

The presidential portraits featured in this book are on exhibit in the Hall of Presidents at the National Portrait Gallery, Smithsonian Institution. Additional illustrative material is drawn primarily from collections at the National Portrait Gallery or the National Museum of American History, Division of Political History.

Much of the campaign memorabilia featured from the National Museum of American History is part of the Becker Collection, a significant group of campaign objects collected and donated by Mr. Ralph Becker.

Complete source information may be found in the Acknowledgments.

A Gramercy Book
distributed by Outlet Book Company, Inc.,
a Random House Company,
225 Park Avenue South,
New York, New York 10003.

Manufactured in the United States of America

Library of Congress Cataloging-in-Publication Data

Voss, Frederick.
The Presidents / Frederick S. Voss.
p.   cm.   —(The Smithsonian treasury)
"A Gramercy book"—CIP t.p. verso.
ISBN 0-517-05950-9
1. Presidents—United States—
History.   2. United States—Politics and
government.   I. Title.   II. Series.
E176.1.V67   1991
353.03′13′0922—dc20   91-3965
                                 CIP

8 7 6 5 4 3 2 1

CONTENTS

INTRODUCTION

The presidency is by far the most influential and prestigious political office in the United States and, because of America's ascendance in the international arena, it is a central focus of world politics as well. As the nation's chief administrator, the holder of this office determines how and when the laws of the country are to be implemented. Given his power of veto over congressional acts and his status as the only public official to be elected by all of the people, he has also come to exercise a substantial and, on occasion, dominant influence on what those laws should be. As the constitutionally designated commander in chief of the country's armed forces, he is charged with overseeing national security against both internal and external threats and, in time of war, that responsibility can vest him with powers that are almost dictatorial in their scope. Finally, as chief diplomat, the president is the primary architect of the policies that determine the country's relationships with the rest of the world.

The powers of the presidency are not, however, unlimited, nor is the holder of this office free to pursue courses strictly according to his own desires. On the contrary, the democratic process of which the president is a part places numerous constraints on his power to act and many a presidential wish has gone unfulfilled in the face of a recalcitrant Congress or a hostile climate of public opinion. Moreover, on many occasions when the president has had his way, the unforeseen negative consequences of his triumph have diminished his credibility and, in turn, his capacity to lead.

The presidency is an enormous job. To carry out its multifaceted responsibilities requires at times more genius, stamina, and foresight than any individual could be expected to possess. It therefore comes as no surprise that over the past two centuries, many of the holders of that office have taken a decidedly negative view of it. Thinking back on his White House years, John Adams once said: "Had I been

chosen President again, I am certain I could not have lived another year." For Adams's successor, Thomas Jefferson, the presidency meant "unceasing drudgery and daily loss of friends," and John Quincy Adams claimed that his presidential term represented "the four most miserable years" of his life. Abraham Lincoln compared his feelings about being president to those of the hapless man who had just been tarred and feathered and ridden out of town on a rail. When someone asked the man what he thought of the experience, he replied, "If it wasn't for the honor of the thing, I'd rather walk." And then there was Grover Cleveland, who, at a particularly troublesome moment late in his first term, took the hand of a young White House visitor named Franklin Roosevelt and said: "My little man, I am making a strange wish for you. It is that you may never be President of the United States."

To some extent, these and many other similar statements made about the presidency by those who have known it most intimately are only expressions of momentary frustrations that anyone might feel in his job. Indeed, some presidents have reveled in the burdens of their office. The most notable was the incurably ebullient Theodore Roosevelt, who once declared that no one "ever enjoyed the presidency as I did." Still, the presidency is an office that has more than the usual potential for causing unhappiness for anyone who attains it. If it were possible to poll the forty men who have occupied the presidency since 1789, perhaps most of them would not summarize their White House years in the unequivocally gloomy terms that John Quincy Adams did. By the same token, however, they would undoubtedly fully understand why he felt that way.

Despite its attendant travails, the presidency has never suffered from a scarcity of applicants. Of his own unceasing, but frustrated, presidential yearnings, Daniel Webster is alleged to have said, "I am but a man, Sir. I want it! I want It! I want it!" Certainly, Webster was not unique in his quadrennial lustings after America's highest office. As long as the presidency continues to be the main focus of political power in the United States, the number of individuals who could say "I want it! I want it! I want it!" will remain ample.

While the plenitude of eager presidential aspirants has long been a constant factor in American political life, other dimensions of the presidency have not been as predictable. Among the more noteworthy of these variables are the biographical profiles of the individuals who have occupied the office.

According to the Constitution, there are only three qualifications that a would-be president has to meet before seeking the office: The individual must be a native-born American; must have been a legal resident of the United States for at least fourteen

7

years; and must be over the age of thirty-five. Beyond that, legally speaking at least, there are no other criteria that must be met. That is not to say, however, that there are no other less explicitly stated barriers to achieving the presidency. Until 1960, for example, it was generally thought that a Catholic could never be president, and it is only recently that the American electorate has shown even vague signs that it might one day accept the notion of putting a woman, an African-American, or a person of Asian descent into the White House.

But even within the limits set by the Constitution and custom, the origin and background of America's presidents have varied considerably. In terms of their education, for example, White House occupants have ranged from the largely self-taught Andrew Johnson, who did not master the basics of writing until early adulthood, to the scholarly Woodrow Wilson, who held a doctor of philosophy degree from Johns Hopkins. With regard to social and economic origin, the variety has been equally striking. In contrast to Theodore and Franklin Roosevelt, who hailed from America's most socially prestigious elite, and John F. Kennedy, who was the son of a multimillionaire, other presidents, including Abraham Lincoln and Dwight Eisenhower, began life under circumstances that could only be described as hardscrabble.

Perhaps a more interesting aspect of presidential diversity is the great range of vocational backgrounds from which these men, the residents of 1600 Pennsylvania Avenue, have come. While Andrew Johnson began life as a humble tailor and Ronald Reagan was for many years a movie actor, the first rung on Herbert Hoover's ladder to the White House was an internationally acclaimed career as a mining engineer. Ulysses S. Grant, in the years immediately following his resignation from the army in 1854, was at one point reduced to pawning his gold watch to see his family through the Christmas holidays. Another example of prepresidential failure was Harry S Truman's ill-starred venture into the men's clothing business, which left him at the age of thirty-eight with a mountain of debt and very poor prospects of ever paying it off.

In contemplating the considerable variety in presidential backgrounds, the question arises: Is there any correlation between a president's past and his performance in the White House? At best, the answer is an ambiguous maybe. In the case of George Washington, for instance, his brilliance as a leader of men through the trying circumstances of the Revolution promised success as his country's first president, and

his presidency did indeed live up to that expectation. Similarly, Lyndon B. Johnson's expertise in bringing his presidential will to bear on Congress can clearly be traced to his many years of experience as the Democratic majority leader of the Senate. In view of Warren Harding's lackluster career in Congress, it is no surprise that he turned out to be one of the weakest presidents.

On the other hand, the United States has had many presidents whose White House behavior and accomplishments were at odds with their pasts. Herbert Hoover's humanitarian instincts, for example, led to his immensely successful efforts to feed the starving civilian masses of Europe during World War I. But in the face of the Great Depression that set in during his presidency, he could not see his way to mounting a similar drive to alleviate the resulting widespread hardships. Chester Arthur was another man whose White House behavior did not square with his prepresidential career. He owed his political existence to the spoils system that had thoroughly corrupted the federal civil service of his day, but after taking office he used his presidential prestige to help abolish that system. A more startling presidential surprise was Franklin Roosevelt, whose reputation as a political trimmer with little taste for reforming adventurism seemed to promise an administration unnoted for innovation. Yet, within days of his inauguration, Roosevelt was rushing headlong into a series of experimental reforms that would redefine dramatically the role of the federal government in American life.

That there is no way to predict how an aspiring candidate will behave when elected is one of the most intriguing aspects of the presidency. Of Andrew Jackson's imminent accession to the presidency in 1829, Daniel Webster wrote, "When he comes, he will bring a breeze with him. . . . Which way it will blow, I cannot tell." That comment could have been made of many presidents as they prepared to undertake their White House responsibilities.

But if anticipating presidential behavior is an uncertain game at best, it is not necessary to go far to discover why. Nothing in a newly elected incumbent's previous experience can fully prepare him for the uniqueness of the presidency and the magnitude of its demands. As a result, until an individual actually experiences the office, even he cannot chart with accuracy the course he will travel. As Lyndon Johnson once said, his presidential duties reminded him of a statement often made by his father: "Son, you will never know what it is to be a father until you *are* a father."

GEORGE WASHINGTON

FIRST PRESIDENT   1789–1797

Of the many likenesses for which George Washington posed, none is better known than the so-called Athenaeum portrait by Gilbert Stuart. Mrs. Washington commissioned the piece, as well as a likeness of herself, and she undoubtedly intended to hang the two pictures at the couple's home at Mount Vernon. Stuart, however, never completed the backgrounds in either picture. Instead he kept them in his studio and used the unfinished portrait of Washington as reference for painting scores of other Washington likenesses for which there was a ready market. The portrait's blood-and-flesh vitality makes the popularity of these replicas understandable.

The medal above commemorates the British evacuation of Boston on March 17, 1776. In a shrewd, strategic move, General George Washington, the commander in chief of the Revolutionary forces, positioned his artillery on Dorchester Heights overlooking Boston, placing the British forces below in an undefendable position. Despite this early victory, it would be five more long and hard years of war until the English surrender at Yorktown.

Included in this engraving of Edward Savage's portrait of the Washingtons are two of Martha's grandchildren, George Washington Parke Custis and Eleanor Parke Custis. In the background is one of the more than three hundred slaves owned by Washington. Early in the 1770s, Washington became committed to gradually abolishing the slave trade through legislation, and he refused to sell slaves he did not need without their permission. Although he compared the tyranny of slavery with that of Britain toward the colonies, he opposed freeing slaves who were content with their masters. On the table there is a map of the Potomac River. Martha is pointing to the site of the new federal capital which was still under construction in 1799 when Washington died, a year after this print was published.

Today, in the United States, a president reaches office after a hard-fought, drawn-out campaign between two major candidates that is marked by heated debate about issues both serious and petty. In the country's first two presidential elections, however, in 1788 and 1792, the mechanisms for determining who would lead did not work that way. On those occasions, George Washington claimed the nation's highest office in contests in which he was virtually the only candidate.

The reason for this anomaly was simple. As commander of the Continental Army during the Revolution, Washington had guided the country to independence. As presiding officer of the Constitutional Convention of 1787, he had also been a major influence when the plans for the federal government were drawn up. Moreover, he had always performed with a dignity and evenhanded forcefulness that had by the late 1780s transformed him in the eyes of his countrymen into a kind of demigod. Thus, when Americans settled down to electing their first president under the newly ratified Constitution, they considered George Washington the only logical choice.

Despite the luster attached to Washington's name, his eight years in the presidency did not pass without criticism. Thomas Jefferson, his secretary of state, remarked, for example, on his fiery temper and his social aloofness that inspired charges of elitism. The Jay Treaty of 1794 with England, which was meant to settle questions largely related to trade and overlapping territorial claims, spawned the accusation that Washington's administration had betrayed American interests. And among the newspaper attacks on policies late in his administration was one describing him as "the scourge and misfortune of our country."

Nevertheless, the election of Washington as first president of the United States was indeed a wise choice. Under his leadership, the new republic achieved a stable and responsible fiscal policy that created a sorely needed climate of assurance for trade and industry. In diplomacy, he adroitly steered the country clear of hazardous hostilities in the Anglo-French conflicts that came in the wake of the French Revolution. Finally, when western Pennsylvanians rebelled over a federal whisky tax, there was no doubt that Washington's decisiveness in the situation demonstrated that the young republic's unity could weather the divisiveness of local unrest. In short, even with benefit of hindsight, there are few historians who would dispute the longstanding assertion that Washington was one of the most effective chief executives the country has ever had.

Perhaps Thomas Jefferson explained this extraordinary presidential success best. On the one hand, he noted that Washington's intellect was by no means "of the very first order." But far outweighing that was Washington's fearlessness, integrity, and sense of justice, which was unmatched among his contemporaries. "He was indeed," Jefferson claimed, "in every sense of the word, a wise, a good, and a great man."

Jefferson might also have added that personal power was never an end in itself for George Washington. Where others might have used a commanding prestige such as his to hold on to the presidency for a third term, he was quite content to retire in 1797, firm in the belief that the need for his services had passed.

BORN
Pope's Creek, Westmoreland County, Virginia,
February 22, 1732

ANCESTRY
English

WIFE
Martha Dandridge Custis
Born: New Kent County, Virginia
June 21, 1731
Died: Mount Vernon, Virginia
May 22, 1802

MARRIED
Kent County, Virginia, January 6, 1759

CHILDREN
Two children adopted from his wife's first marriage

HOME
Mount Vernon, Virginia

EDUCATION
Tutored at home

RELIGION
Episcopalian

OCCUPATIONS
Surveyor, soldier, and planter

MILITARY SERVICE
Rose from major to colonel, Virginia militia (1752-1758)
Commander in Chief of Continental Army (1775-1783)

PREPRESIDENTIAL OFFICES
Member of the Virginia House of Burgesses (1759-1774)
Justice of Fairfax County (1768-1774)
Delegate to the First and Second Continental Congresses
(1774-1775)
President of the Constitutional Convention (1787)

POLITICAL PARTY
Federalist

INAUGURATED AS PRESIDENT
First term: April 30, 1789, Federal Hall, New York City
Second term: March 4, 1793, Federal Hall, Philadelphia

AGE AT INAUGURATION
57

DIED
Mount Vernon, December 14, 1799, age 67

JOHN ADAMS

As vice-president, John Adams believed that the bestowing of dignified titles on officials in the United States' new federal government was a small but essential part of winning respect for its authority. Consequently, he urged the Senate to endorse titles of a rather exalting nature. As John Trumbull's portrait indicates, the rounded features of the short and stout Adams made him an easy mark for derision in this discussion. Soon the more democratically minded senators were referring to him as "His Rotundity."

By John Adams's own account he was "puffy, vain, conceited." Abigail Smith Adams, pictured above at the age of fifty-six, was a well-read woman who never hesitated to speak her mind and supported Adams as he emerged as a public figure. She dealt lightly with his hypochondria and premonitions of an early death during a marriage which lasted for more than fifty years.

On November 1, 1800, John Adams became the first president to sleep in the newly erected White House. Adams wrote this prayer, which Franklin Roosevelt had engraved on the mantle of the State Dining Room almost one hundred and fifty years later: "I pray Heaven to bestow the best Blessings on this House and all that shall inhabit it. May none but honest and wise men ever rule under this roof." This photolithograph after a painting by N. C. Wyeth was done early in the twentieth century.

When John Adams took up his duties as George Washington's vice-president in 1789, he found that his responsibilities were few and generally unimportant. No matter how he tried, he realized the position would never carry much weight, and he soon confessed to his wife that he now occupied "the most insignificant office that ever the invention of man contrived."

The proud Adams brooded over this situation as he performed his duties as the Senate's presiding officer. In the course of his brooding, it undoubtedly crossed his mind that this was a poor way indeed for a country to reward a man of his distinction. Such a thought was not unwarranted. One of the most effective opponents to British rule in the decade preceding the Revolution, John Adams served his country well when war came in 1775. As a member of the committee appointed to draft the Declaration of Independence, he was one of its most articulate supporters. Adams also played a part in negotiating the Anglo-American treaty of 1783, officially ending the Revolution, and he served as the United States' first minister to the Court of St. James.

Unjustly neglected though he might have felt, Vice-President Adams nevertheless must have taken comfort in the knowledge that he was the most likely successor to Washington's presidency. He was not disappointed. Had he known, however, of the storms ahead, he might not have been at all pleased with this turn of events.

At the heart of Adams's presidential difficulties were relations with the new republican regime in France, which in its war with Britain and other European powers had been interfering with America's transatlantic shipping. In dealing with this problem, he found himself besieged on one side by a vocal segment within his own Federalist party that was rabidly hostile to the French. On the other side, he faced the pro-French Anti-Federalists, who believed that because of America's republican ideology, the country's leaders were obliged to do everything in their power to advance France's cause against European royalists. Unfortunately, Adams's attempt to keep the country out of the imbroglios of Europe, while still maintaining its shipping rights as a neutral nation, satisfied neither side. Everything came to a head in 1798. Out of the diplomatic mission Adams dispatched that year to Paris came the notorious "XYZ affair" in which the French refused to begin talks on United States shipping rights until Adams's emissaries had granted them a substantial loan. The insult engendered a protest from anti-French Federalists that was both instant and deafening. When Adams ultimately rejected their urgings of war with France in favor of continuing to press for a negotiated settlement, this anger was directed at him.

Adams also came under fire because of the Alien and Sedition Acts. Passed to curb French interference in American domestic affairs, these laws were a significant infringement on free speech. In this matter, Adams drew scorn from both Federalists and Anti-Federalists. While Anti-Federalists took his administration to task for implementing these measures at all, Federalists criticized its failure to apply them stringently.

Leaving the presidency in 1801, the much-battered Adams retired to his farm in Quincy, Massachusetts. Shortly thereafter, he remarked that he had not been so happy "since some sin unknown to me involved me in politics."

BORN
Quincy, Massachusetts, October 30, 1735

ANCESTRY
English

WIFE
Abigail Smith
Born: Weymouth, Massachusetts
November 23, 1744
Died: Quincy, Massachusetts
October 28, 1818

MARRIED
Weymouth, Massachusetts, October 25, 1764

CHILDREN
Abigail Amelia (1765-1813)
John Quincy (1767-1848)
Susanna (1768-1770)
Charles (1770-1800)
Thomas Boylston (1772-1832)

HOME
Peacefield, Quincy, Massachusetts

EDUCATION
Harvard University, Cambridge, Massachusetts; B.A.
(1755),
M.A. (1758)

RELIGION
Unitarian

OCCUPATIONS
Teacher, farmer, lawyer, and writer

PREPRESIDENTIAL OFFICES
Representative to the Massachusetts General Court (1770)
Delegate to the First and Second Continental Congresses
(1774-1777)
Member of the Provincial Congress of Massachusetts
(1770-1774)
Delegate to the Massachusetts Constitutional Convention
(1779)
Minister to France (1779-1782)
Minister to the Netherlands (1782-1785)
Minister to England (1785-1788)
Vice-President (1789-1796)

POLITICAL PARTY
Federalist

INAUGURATED AS PRESIDENT
March 4, 1797, Federal Hall, Philadelphia

AGE AT INAUGURATION
61

DIED
Quincy, Massachusetts, July 4, 1826, age 90

THOMAS JEFFERSON

THIRD PRESIDENT   1801–1809

In 1805, Thomas Jefferson commissioned and posed for this portrait by Gilbert Stuart. The foremost portraitist of the early American republic, Stuart relished nothing more than painting a face. But he found the completion of the background elements of his likenesses tedious. As a result, he was often late in delivering his pictures. Jefferson, for example, waited sixteen years for this picture, and even when it arrived at Monticello in 1821, it was not entirely finished.

On this portable desk, Jefferson wrote the first draft of the Declaration of Independence in June 1776. Of the document and its importance Jefferson stated ". . . we were not acting for ourselves alone but for the whole human race . . . to show whether man can be trusted with self-government."

In 1782, after visiting Monticello, pictured in the photoengraving, left, the Marquis de Chastellux commented that Jefferson was "the first American who has consulted the Fine Arts to know how he should shelter himself from the weather." Jefferson not only designed the thirty-two-room house and the elaborate gardens, but he invented such devices for it as folding ladders, a dumbwaiter on which food and wine could be brought from the cellar, swivel chairs, and alcove beds. But for Jefferson, Monticello was more than an exercise in architecture and invention, it was the center of his existence.

In 1962, President John F. Kennedy looked out over a White House gathering of Nobel prize winners and declared, "I think this is the most extraordinary collection of talent, of human knowledge, that has ever been gathered together at the White House with the possible exception of when Thomas Jefferson dined alone."

Never before or since Thomas Jefferson's presidency has a man of such remarkable versatility occupied the office. As author of the Declaration of Independence, he gave the world what may be its most compelling defense of liberty and political self-determination. As a staunch advocate of the power of education, he fathered the University of Virginia and as a self-taught architect he designed its wonderful colonnaded buildings. At his Monticello plantation in Virginia, he created one of the most beautiful homes ever built in the United States. As an inventor, he produced a host of ingenious contrivances and, as a naturalist, he promoted the early investigations of North America's natural environment.

Yet, despite his varied talents, Jefferson's presidency was at best a mixed success. While his first term yielded several noteworthy triumphs, the second left him vulnerable to bitter attacks.

On the positive side was the acquisition of the trans-Mississippi wilderness known as the Louisiana Purchase. Jefferson's narrow interpretation of the Constitution made him doubt his power to obtain this territory without consulting Congress. But, when Napoleon offered it in 1803 at a bargain price, he had the sense to snap it up before the French emperor changed his mind. He also had the wisdom to follow up this lucky stroke by dispatching the Lewis and Clark expedition to discover the new territory's potential and record its natural features.

The early years of Jefferson's administration also marked the solution of an irksome problem facing American shipping —the pirates of Africa's Barbary Coast who routinely extorted handsome fees in exchange for safe passage through the Mediterranean. Again Jefferson had to overcome his scruples—in this case his pacifism—to deal with the situation. But overcome them he did. After sending the navy to the Mediterranean on a mission of armed intimidation, the United States extracted from the Barbary state of Tripoli a treaty highly favorable to its trading interests.

Jefferson was decidedly less successful, however, in confronting Britain and France, which, in their war with each other, both claimed the right to seize American trading vessels bound for enemy ports. Jefferson's solution on this occasion was the Embargo Act of 1807, which halted all foreign commerce. This Draconian measure never achieved its aim of coercing Britain and France to respect the rights of the United States as a neutral nation, but it did result in enormous hardships for American citizens. As for Jefferson himself, the embargo evoked a popular wrath that quite obscured his earlier successes and undoubtedly made all the sweeter his retirement in 1809 from what he termed "the splendid misery" of the presidency.

BORN
Shadwell, Albemarle County, Virginia, April 13, 1743

ANCESTRY
Welsh

WIFE
Martha Wayles Skelton
Born: Charles City County, Virginia
October 30, 1748
Died: Monticello, Charlottesville, Virginia
September 6, 1782

MARRIED
The Forest, Charles City County, Virginia, January 1, 1772

CHILDREN
Martha (1772-1836)
Maria (1778-1804)
Lucy Elizabeth (1782-1785)
Two daughters and one son who died in infancy

HOME
Monticello, Charlottesville, Virginia

EDUCATION
College of William and Mary, Williamsburg, Virginia;
B.A. (1762)

RELIGION
No denomination

OCCUPATIONS
Planter, lawyer, writer, philosopher, scientist,
architect, and educator

PREPRESIDENTIAL OFFICES
Member of the Virginia House of Burgesses (1769-1774)
Deputy Delegate to the Second Continental Congress
(1775-1776)
Member of the Virginia House of Delegates (1776-1779)
Governor of Virginia (1779-1781)
Delegate to the Continental Congress (1783-1784)
Commissioner to France (1784-1785)
Minister to France (1785-1789)
Secretary of State (1790-1793)
Vice-President (1797-1801)

POLITICAL PARTY
Democratic-Republican

INAUGURATED AS PRESIDENT
First term: March 4, 1801, Senate Chamber of the Capitol,
Washington D.C.
Second term: March 4, 1805, Senate Chamber of the
Capitol, Washington, D.C.

AGE AT INAUGURATION
57

DIED
Monticello, Charlottesville, Virginia, July 4, 1826,
age 83

JAMES MADISON

FOURTH PRESIDENT   1809–1817

James Madison posed for this portrait in about 1829, the year he came out of retirement to attend a convention called to revise Virginia's state constitution. Although he was nearing eighty and suffering from the frailties of age, this reentry into the public arena rejuvenated him. According to one observer, "His abundant stock of racy anecdotes were the delight of every social board."

In sharp contrast to her serious and often reticent husband, Dolley Madison was vivacious and outgoing. Somewhat at odds with her Quaker upbringing, she took snuff and was said to "rouge." Her lavish teas, lawn parties, and dinners at the White House were renowned for their gay spontaneity. During the War of 1812, shortly before British troops burned the city of Washington, it was she who rescued from imminent destruction the White House's Gilbert Stuart portrait of George Washington, as well as a number of important government documents. The portrait of Mrs. Madison above, was painted by William S. Elwell in 1848, a year before her death.

On September 10, 1813, the American fleet on Lake Erie led by Master Commandant Oliver Hazard Perry, right, routed and captured a larger English fleet in one of the most decisive battles of the War of 1812. Perry's declaration on that occasion, "We have met the enemy and they are ours," became a patriotic battle cry that rallied flagging popular support for Madison and the war, which had, until then, been going disastrously for the United States.

"very Person seems to acknowledge his greatness. He blends together the profound politician with the Scholar. In the management of every great question he evidently took the lead in the Convention, and tho' he cannot be called an Orator, he is a most agreeable, eloquent, and convincing Speaker. . . . The affairs of the United States, he perhaps has the most knowledge of, of any Man in the Union." That is the way one of his fellow delegates described the diminutive James Madison as he appeared at the United States Constitutional Convention of 1787. But flattering though these words were, they did not do the Virginian full justice.

Known today as the Father of the Constitution, James Madison had long deplored the weaknesses of the central government that had been established under the Articles of Confederation following the Revolution. It had been his proddings, as much as anything, that had led to the Constitutional Convention and a second attempt to create a strong political union among the states. It was Madison who also inspired the so-called Virginia Plan that served as the invaluable springboard for the convention's debates. And, in the battle for the Constitution's ratification following the convention, no one worked more effectively to win its popular acceptance.

As president under the Constitution that he sired, however, Madison was not nearly so successful. Inheriting the problem of British and French interference in American shipping from the Jefferson administration, he never managed to find a peaceful solution to that thorny issue. Instead, clever French maneuvering eventually coalesced with British encroachments on the country's western frontiers to create the perception that Britain was by far the worst of the two violators of America's shipping trade. Consequently, the growing anti-English sentiment had forced Madison to declare war on Britain.

Madison proved to be a poor wartime administrator. Among other things, he took the country into conflict at a moment when it was ill-prepared, and he was inexplicably slow to remedy the situation by appointing capable military leaders. As a result, the war went badly for the United States and for Madison. By the time the British burned the nation's capital in 1814, his popularity was severely diminished. In many quarters, especially in New England where the War of 1812 had been opposed from the start, the conflict was bitterly characterized as "Mr. Madison's War."

Still more potentially hurtful to Madison's waning reputation was the Treaty of Ghent, which finally brought the nation peace, but also left unsatisfied most of the grievances the war was intended to redress. But news of the treaty, which in effect turned the war into a costly draw, inspired no angry move to drive Madison out of the nation's charred capital. Instead, he soon found himself largely restored to the public's good graces.

This was due in part to the constructiveness of Madison's final two years in the White House. It was also the result of the nationalistic pride that came with several battlefield triumphs in the war, the most notable of which was Andrew Jackson's dramatic victory at the Battle of New Orleans. When the public celebrated the triumph of Jackson and other war heroes, they also made a place in that pantheon for Madison, the little man who had dared to take on the British Goliath.

James Madison

BORN
Port Conway, Virginia, March 16, 1751

ANCESTRY
English

WIFE
Dorothea (Dolly) Payne Todd
Born: Guilford County, North Carolina
May 20, 1768
Died: Washington, D.C.
July 12, 1849

MARRIED
Harewood, Virginia, September 15, 1794

CHILDREN
None

HOME
Montpelier, Virginia

EDUCATION
Princeton University, Princeton, New Jersey; B.A. (1771)
One year postgraduate study at Princeton (1771-1772)

RELIGION
Episcopalian

OCCUPATION OTHER THAN PRESIDENCY
Politician

PREPRESIDENTIAL OFFICES
Member of the Orange County Committee of Safety (1774)
Delegate to the the Virginia Convention (1776)
Member of the Virginia Legislature (1776-1777)
Member of the Virginia Executive Council (1778-1779)
Delegate to the Continental Congress
(1780-1783 and 1787-1788)
Member of the Virginia House of Delegates
(1784-1786 and 1799-1800)
Delegate to the Annapolis Convention (1786)
Delegate to the Constitutional Convention (1787)
Member of the Virginia Ratification Convention (1788)
Member of the U.S. House of Representatives (1789-1797)
Secretary of State (1801-1809)

INAUGURATED AS PRESIDENT
First term: March 4, 1809, House of Representatives,
Washington, D.C.
Second term: March 4, 1813, House of Representatives,
Washington, D.C.

POLITICAL PARTY
Democratic-Republican

AGE AT INAUGURATION
57

DIED
Montpelier, Virginia, June 28, 1836, age 85

JAMES MONROE

FIFTH PRESIDENT 1817–1825

James Monroe had a decided taste for things French and during his presidency the White House was largely refurbished with pieces he had acquired during his diplomatic assignments in France. When Monroe commissioned this portrait in 1816, it was not surprising that the artist he selected to paint it was John Vanderlyn, one of the few American painters of the day who had been trained in France.

The mug pictured above, with Monroe's named misspelled, commemorates his enduring presidential popularity. Even the financial panic of 1819 did not prevent his reelection in 1820, which would have been unanimous in the Electoral College except for one dissenting ballot.

Elizabeth Kortright Monroe was a stately and reserved First Lady who attempted to make the White House a grandiose court, replacing Dolley Madison's spontaneous style with formal protocol. Mrs. Monroe presided over White House social occasions with a regal air. And unlike her predecessors, she neither returned calls nor received casual visitors. Despite her aloofness, she did on occasion play an important part in her husband's public life. When Monroe was minister to France, for example, she complied with his request that she demonstrate American disapproval of the imprisonment of the wife of the Marquis de Lafayette, during the Reign of Terror, by visiting her in prison. Shortly after this much publicized event the authorities released Madame Lafayette.

In 1819, there was a financial panic in the United States followed by much personal suffering. Although such an event might be expected to spell disaster for the White House incumbent who presided over it and thwart whatever hopes he might have for reelection, in the case of President James Monroe's bid for a second term in 1820, the recent economic calamity had no negative impact. To the contrary, he became that year the only presidential candidate, other than George Washington, to gain office virtually unopposed.

The reasons for this turn of events did not lie in a compelling personality, for in truth Monroe was a rather dry and colorless individual. He was, however, the last of the so-called Virginia Dynasty that included Washington, Jefferson, and Madison and that had played such a crucial role in the nation's early history. Although Monroe's own part had been minor, compared to those of the three other men, it was not negligible. As an officer in the Revolution, he had nursed the wounds of the great Lafayette and figured prominently in the defeat of the British at the Battle of Trenton. During Washington's and Jefferson's administrations, he had served as a diplomat, and under Madison, he had performed admirably as secretary of both the War and State Departments.

Monroe's connection to the Virginia Dynasty accounted only in part for his electoral success in 1820. His unopposed candidacy was, above all, a result of the Era of Good Feelings that set in after the War of 1812, and that was marked by a surging nationalism and the temporary halt of two-party factionalism.

Monroe brought to the presidency a temporizing outlook that meshed well with the Era of Good Feelings. When, for example, heated congressional controversy over the admission of Missouri as a slave state ended in a compromise, admitting Missouri while banning slavery in other western territories, Monroe questioned its constitutionality. But rather than risk fueling animosity between the country's pro-slavery and abolitionist factions, he signed the bill into law. Similarly, when he vetoed a bill calling for federal improvements in transportation on the ground that it was unconstitutional, he sought to placate the bill's supporters by suggesting legislative strategies for satisfying his objections.

The best-remembered achievements of Monroe's presidency, however, were in the field of foreign policy, and he capped his first term with the acquisition of Florida from Spain in 1819. Four years later, with rumors that there was scheming in Europe to help Spain regain dominion over Latin American countries that had recently won their independence from her, Monroe gave voice to a doctrine that would forever bear his name.

The occasion was his seventh annual message to Congress, in which he stated that the United States would not tolerate European tampering with the sovereignty of states in any of the Americas. Actually authored by Secretary of State John Quincy Adams, the Monroe Doctrine did not have any immediate impact, since the threats from Europe had no real substance. But as the years passed, situations arose in which Monroe's successors found it useful to invoke his doctrine as justification for their actions. Today, many Americans regard the Monroe Doctrine as an immutable article of their national faith.

James Monroe

BORN
Westmoreland County, Virginia, April 28, 1758

ANCESTRY
Scottish

WIFE
Elizabeth Kortright
Born: New York City, New York
June 30, 1768
Died: Oak Hill, Loudon County, Virginia
September, 23, 1830

MARRIED
New York City, New York, February 16, 1786

CHILDREN
Eliza (1787-1835?)
Maria Hester (1804-1850)

HOMES
Ash Lawn, Charlottesville, Virginia
Oak Hill, Loudon County, Virginia

EDUCATION
Attended College of William and Mary,
Williamsburg, Virginia (1774-1775)

RELIGION
Episcopalian

OCCUPATIONS
Lawyer and writer

MILITARY SERVICE
Rose from lieutenant to major, Third Virginia Regiment
and Continental Army (1775-1779)
Military Commissioner for Virginia Army (1780-1782)

PREPRESIDENTIAL OFFICES
Representative to the Virginia Legislature (1782-1783)
Representative to the Continental Congress (1783-1786)
Representative to the Virginia Assembly
(1786-1787 and 1810-1811)
Member of the U.S. Senate (1790-1794)
Minister to France (1794-1796)
Minister to England (1803-1807)
Governor of Virginia (1799-1802 and 1811)
Secretary of War (1814-1815)
Secretary of State (1811-1814 and 1815-1817)

POLITICAL PARTY
Democratic-Republican

INAUGURATED AS PRESIDENT
First term: March 4, 1817, the Capitol, Washington, D.C.
Second term: March 5, 1821, House of Representatives,
Washington, D.C.

AGE AT INAUGURATION
58

DIED
New York City, New York, July 4, 1831, age 73

JOHN QUINCY ADAMS

SIXTH PRESIDENT   1825–1829

It is believed that this portrait of John Quincy Adams by George Caleb Bingham is one of several likenesses derived from sittings that Adams had with the artist in Washington in 1844. Adams confided in his diary that he did not think that Bingham was "likely to make . . . either a strong likeness or a fine picture." But the artist seems to have done both. In its stoic vitality, the portrait is almost a visual echo of Ralph Waldo Emerson's written description of Adams as an old man. "When they talk about his . . . nearness to the grave," Emerson remarked, "he knows better. He is like one of those old cardinals, who quick as he is chosen Pope, throws away his crutches . . . and is straight as a boy."

John Quincy Adams spent the last eighteen years of his public life in the House of Representatives. On February 21, 1848, he suffered a stroke while seated in the House and was carried to the Speakers Room where he died two days later. He regained consciousness only once to say, "Thank the officers of the House. This is the last of earth. I am content." Thomas Hart Benton, an old adversary of Adams, commented, "Where could death have found him but at the post of duty?"

Andrew Jackson's backers were outraged that John Quincy Adams claimed the presidency in the 1824 election even though Jackson had won a larger popular vote. To keep this anger alive and galvanize Jacksonites to elect their man to the White House in 1828, a potter produced this crock inscribed with a legend asserting that Jackson had won a majority of the vote in the four-way contest of 1824. In fact, he had claimed only a plurality.

Of the four candidates—Andrew Jackson, John Quincy Adams, William Crawford, and Henry Clay—who sought the presidency in the campaign of 1824, Jackson clearly garnered the most popular votes. Unfortunately for Jackson, however, his plurality did not give him the majority in the Electoral College that was needed to put him in office. As the Constitution requires in such situations, the task of choosing the nation's next president from among the four candidates was, therefore, left to the House of Representatives, which ultimately selected John Quincy Adams.

Unfortunately for Adams, however, this victory was not untainted. For he owed his election to a political horse trade; he had bought the votes of Henry Clay's supporters in the House by promising to make Clay his secretary of state. Thus, with Jackson's followers crying "Corrupt Bargain" and swearing to even the score at the next election, Adams embarked on his administration under a cloud that challenged its very legitimacy.

Another man might have been able to rise above that cloud. But not Adams. Aloof, rigid, and often tactlessly abrupt, this son of the nation's second president was poorly suited for the political game of compromise and conciliation. Consequently, when Congress balked at his proposals for such things as a comprehensive national transportation system and a means for regulating the country's resources, he proved incapable of changing its mind.

Adams's presidency, however, was not completely without accomplishments. By the time he left office, after his defeat by Jackson in the election of 1828, he had secured congressional approval of funding for the Chesapeake and Ohio Canal as well as several commercial agreements with European powers. Nevertheless, these were small triumphs when measured against his administration's many failed hopes.

When weighing Adams's presidential failures against his success in other phases of his career, however, their significance also shrinks. As minister to the Netherlands and Prussia in the 1790s he had been an unusually able representative of American interests. Still more impressive was his record as James Monroe's secretary of state, and many historians claim that Adams might rank as the country's most effective secretary of state. But of the several public roles he played, perhaps the most interesting came after his retirement from the presidency.

Contrary to his pathetic declaration that "the sun of my political life sets in deepest gloom," Adams's sun was not even close to setting when he left the White House in early 1829. In the year following, he won election to the House of Representatives, where he sat for eighteen years. Predictably, his stubborn inflexibility prevented Adams from becoming a major power broker in Congress. On one issue, however, this quality made him effective. Thanks to his dogged efforts over many years, in 1844, the House finally repealed its "gag rule," which had prohibited it from accepting citizen petitions condemning southern slavery. The repeal campaign made Adams the object of bitter hatred in the South, but among northern abolitionists he became affectionately known as "Old Man Eloquent."

John Quincy Adams

BORN
Quincy, Massachusetts, July 11, 1767

ANCESTRY
English

FATHER
John Adams, the second president

WIFE
Louisa Catherine Johnson
Born: London, England
February 12, 1775
Died: Washington, D.C.
May 15, 1852

MARRIED
London, England, July 26, 1797

CHILDREN
George Washington (1801-1829)
John (1803-1834)
Charles Francis (1807-1886)
Louisa Catherine (1811-1812)

EDUCATION
Harvard University, Cambridge, Massachusetts; B.A. (1787)
Studied law with Theophilus Parsons of Newburyport,
Massachusetts (1787-1790)

RELIGION
Unitarian

OCCUPATIONS
Lawyer, professor, and writer

PREPRESIDENTIAL OFFICES
Minister to the Netherlands (1794-1797)
Minister to Prussia (1797-1801)
Member of the Massachusetts Senate (1802)
Member of the U.S. Senate (1803-1808)
Minister to Russia (1809-1814)
Minister to Great Britain (1815-1817)
Secretary of State (1817-1825)

POLITICAL PARTY
Federalist until 1808
Democratic-Republican until 1825
National Republican (Whig) thereafter

INAUGURATED AS PRESIDENT
March 4, 1825, Hall of the House of Representatives,
Washington, D.C.

AGE AT INAUGURATION
57

POSTPRESIDENTIAL OFFICES
Member of the U.S. House of Representatives (1831-1848)

DIED
Washington, D.C., February 23, 1848, age 80

ANDREW JACKSON

SEVENTH PRESIDENT   1829–1837

This portrait of Andrew Jackson shows him dressed in the epauletted coat that he may have worn at the Battle of New Orleans. Faintly perceptible in the left background is an equestrian figure meant to represent him as he appeared leading that battle. The artist, Ralph Earl, was one of Jackson's warmest admirers. Shortly after painting his first portrait of Jackson in 1817, he became part of Jackson's household and eventually was known as Jackson's "court painter." As such, one of his main tasks was to fill the demand from Jacksonites for likenesses of their hero.

This cartoon, captioned "The Rats leaving a Falling House," satirizes the resignation of Andrew Jackson's cabinet in 1831, a crisis caused by the scandal surrounding the marriage of John Eaton, the secretary of war, to a vivacious, young widow. Because of the new Mrs. Eaton's reputation in the past for promiscuity, Washington society ostracized the couple even though Jackson and Secretary of State Martin Van Buren defended them. Vice-President John C. Calhoun, vying with Van Buren to be the next president, saw this as an opportunity to discredit Van Buren. He, therefore, encouraged his wife to lead the campaign against the Eatons and so contributed to animosity within the Cabinet that severely hampered its effectiveness. The solution came when first Van Buren and then Eaton resigned, allowing Jackson to ask for the resignations of the rest of the Cabinet, including Calhoun's supporters, thereby ending the controversy with a reorganized Jackson Cabinet and Van Buren in ascendance.

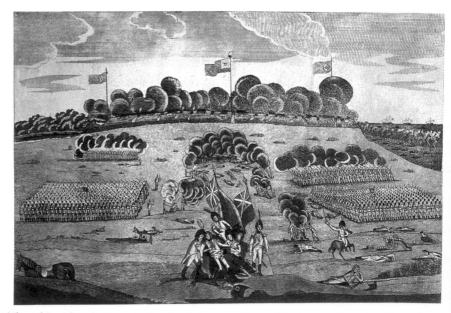

The etching above by Francisco Scacki, A Correct View of the Battle Near the City of New Orleans . . . depicts the final battle of the War of 1812. On January 8, 1815, a large, well-drilled British force sustained 2,036 casualties attacking Jackson's troops, which sustained about forty. This victory electrified the American people and made Jackson a national hero.

In 1828, Andrew Jackson's reputation rested mainly on his fame as the frontier general who in the War of 1812 had defeated the British at the Battle of New Orleans. That year as the campaign to make him president gained momentum, his opponents were therefore deeply troubled that the electorate might be able to place a man in the White House merely because of his military record. But even more disturbing to the conservative, propertied interests who made up much of Jackson's opposition were the populist sentiments that his supporters invoked in their appeals to the voters. As a result, the anti-Jacksonians of 1828 had fearful visions of a new administration that would succumb to the mercurial will of the rabble.

When Jackson triumphed at the polls and his inauguration turned Washington into a town overrun by hordes of rustically mannered celebrants, it seemed that this nightmare had become reality. Indeed, it appeared to many conservatives that the well-being of the United States was about to be undone now that its fate lay in the hands of a leader all too willing to cater to the rank and file.

Of course, Jackson's White House years did not mark the onset of the country's ruination. But that was scant comfort to his critics. Just as they had feared, the hallmark of Jackson's two terms was the use of his presidential powers to challenge, in the name of the people, the nation's vested commercial and financial interests. In 1830, for example, he vetoed a congressional public roads bill on the ground that it would benefit only a few. Two years later, claiming that the Bank of the United States was the creature of a privileged elite, he invoked his veto power again to block the congressional rechartering of that institution.

In thwarting such measures, Jackson incensed his critics on two counts. First, they claimed that he was jeopardizing the nation's economic stability and potential for growth. Second, in contrast to his more circumspect predecessors, he had dared to offer rationales for his vetoes that were not related to constitutional interpretation and, in the process, had turned the presidency into a monarchical dictatorship. Thus, as his opponents coalesced into the new Whig party, in preparation for their unsuccessful bid to oust him in 1832, their favorite cartoon became one portraying Jackson as the Constitution-trampling "King Andrew the First." In light of the president's refusal to implement a Supreme Court ruling concerning the Cherokee Indians in Georgia, such imagery seemed all the more justified.

But while conservatives fumed about Jackson, the nation's farmers and laborers gave him their unflagging loyalty and hailed him as "the greatest man of the age." The most important consequence of Jackson's administration, however, was not his popularity with the common man. Rather it lay in the fact that his aggressive use of his powers had set a precedent that later presidents would expand upon.

Andrew Jackson

BORN
The Waxhaws, South Carolina, March 15, 1767

ANCESTRY
Scottish-Irish

WIFE
Rachel Donelson Robards
Born: Halifax County, Virginia
June 15, 1767
Died: Nashville, Tennessee
December 22, 1828

MARRIED
Natchez, Mississippi, August 1, 1791
Second ceremony in Nashville, Tennessee, January 17, 1794

CHILDREN
Andrew Jackson, Jr. (1810-18 ?)

HOME
The Hermitage, Nashville, Tennessee

EDUCATION
Studied law in Salisbury, South Carolina (1784-1787)

RELIGION
Presbyterian

OCCUPATIONS
Lawyer, soldier, and politician

MILITARY SERVICE
Judge advocate of Davidson County militia (c. 1791)
Major general, Tennessee militia (1802-1813)
Major general, U.S. Army (1814-1821)

PREPRESIDENTIAL OFFICES
Attorney General of Western District of North Carolina (1788-1796)
Delegate to the Tennessee States Constitutional Convention (1796)
Member of the U.S. House of Representatives (1796-1797)
Member of the U.S. Senate (1797-1798 and 1823-1825)
Tennessee Supreme Court Judge (1798-1804)
Governor of Florida Territory (1821)

POLITICAL PARTY
Democratic

INAUGURATED AS PRESIDENT
First Term: March 4, 1829, the Capitol, Washington, D.C.
Second Term: March 4, 1833, House of Representatives, Washington, D.C.

AGE AT INAUGURATION
61

DIED
Nashville, Tennessee, June 8, 1845, age 78

MARTIN VAN BUREN

EIGHTH PRESIDENT   1837–1841

By the time Martin Van Buren posed for this daguerreotype at Matthew Brady's studio, he had long since lost most of his influence in national politics. But his inability to sway minds on public issues of the day did not keep him from taking an interest in them. A long-time opponent of slavery, he was deeply disturbed at the moment by the South's push to extend slaveholding ever farther into America's western territories.

These are two views of a "pull card," a clever Van Buren campaign device from the election of 1840. The figure at left smiles and holds a goblet marked with Van Buren's initials; the caption reads, "A Beautiful Goblet of White House Champagne." When a tab is pulled the frowning face is revealed. William Harrison's initials are on the goblet, with the caption "An Ugly Mug of Log Cabin Hard Cider," referring to Harrison's campaign.

The Democrats chose Kentuckian Richard Mentor Johnson, right, to be Van Buren's vice-presidential running mate in 1836 largely because his frontier origins would attract voters in the West. But Johnson's open cohabitation with a mulatto woman offended many southerners, and when his domestic arrangements prompted Virginia to deny him its electoral votes, he fell short of the majority needed to place him in office. Following the procedure dictated by the 12th Amendment, the Senate, for the first and only time in its history, was called upon to elect the vice-president—and it chose Johnson. A talented soldier in his younger days, Johnson had gained considerable popularity during his terms in the Kentucky legislature and the House of Representatives as the workingman's champion. In the vice-presidency, however, his careless dress and crude manner while presiding over the Senate embarrassed many fellow Democrats. As a result, in Van Buren's quest for a second term, in 1840, he dropped Johnson as his running mate. Johnson became a vice-presidential candidate nevertheless and was defeated.

A former governor of New York, secretary of state under Jackson, and later his vice-president, Martin Van Buren was Jackson's handpicked successor, and he rode into the White House in 1837 on the shirttail of his enormously popular predecessor. But the goodwill engendered by his close association with Jackson did not last long. When Van Buren left the presidency four years later, he was a discredited man.

In many respects the sharp decline in Van Buren's reputation was undeserved. Today, many historians claim that Van Buren was a much more able chief executive than his contemporaries judged him to be. Among his presidential accomplishments, for example, was an eminently sound plan for an independent federal treasury system, which he eventually pushed through Congress in an effort to restore the nation's financial stability following the great economic downturn of 1837. He also had the good sense to ignore cries that he was a tool of British imperialism and to stand by his conviction that Americans must take no part in fomenting civil unrest in Canada over British rule. To Van Buren's credit, too, was his mandate for shortening the work day for laborers employed on federal work projects.

What seems in retrospect to be a quite respectable presidential performance, however, was largely unacknowledged in Van Buren's own day. In good part this was the result of the economic depression that set in with unprecedented severity soon after he took office. Like most presidents who preside over the nation in such circumstances, he was blamed for that misfortune and was soon known as "Martin Van Ruin." Then, too, in 1840, as his Whig opposition geared itself to block his bid for a second term, some of the very campaign strategies that he had exploited so cleverly in helping to put Jackson in the White House in 1828 were used against him.

In much the same way that Van Buren had painted Jackson as the man of the people pitted against the nation's rapacious elitists, the Whigs now began casting Van Buren in the part of the "lily-fingered" aristocrat. Against the backdrop of the continuing depression, the ploy worked well. Thus, when the Whigs used Van Buren's dapper tastes in clothing and an expenditure of several thousand dollars to refurbish the White House as the springboard for depicting him as a perfumed, wine-sipping dandy, the impact was devastating. And when they contrasted this luxury-loving Van Buren with the alleged homespun simplicity of their own presidential hopeful, William Henry Harrison, it became all the more destructive. "Let Van from his coolers of silver drink wine," one Whig ditty began, "And lounge on his cushioned settee; / Our man on his buckeye bench can recline, / Content with hard cider is he!"

Naturally, Van Buren resented this treatment by the Whigs. But when it resulted in his defeat at the polls, he remained the model of courtesy. When Harrison arrived in Washington to take office, Van Buren offered to ease the presidential transition by vacating the White House early. He was also the first defeated incumbent president to pay a call on his successor.

BORN
Kinderhook, New York, December 5, 1782

ANCESTRY
Dutch

WIFE
Hannah Hoes
Born: Kinderhook, New York
March 8, 1783
Died: Albany, New York
February 5, 1819

MARRIED
Catskill, New York, February 21, 1807

CHILDREN
Abraham (1807-1873)
John (1810-1866)
Martin (1812-1855)
Smith Thompson (1817-1876)

HOME
Lindenwald, Kinderhook, New York

EDUCATION
Studied in the law office of Francis Silvester,
Kinderhook, New York (1796-1801)

RELIGION
Dutch Reform

OCCUPATIONS
Lawyer and politician

PREPRESIDENTIAL OFFICES
Surrogate of Columbia County, New York (1808-1813)
Member of the New York State Senate (1813-1820)
Attorney General of New York (1815-1819)
Delegate to the Third New York State Constitutional
Convention (1821)
Member of the U.S. Senate (1821-1828)
Governor of New York (1829)
Secretary of State (1829-1831)
Vice-President (1833-1837)

POLITICAL PARTY
Democratic during Presidency
Free-Soil from 1848

INAUGURATED AS PRESIDENT
March 4, 1837, the Capitol, Washington, D.C.

AGE AT INAUGURATION
54

DIED
Kinderhook, New York, July 24, 1862, age 79

WILLIAM HENRY HARRISON

NINTH PRESIDENT   1841

During his presidential campaign, William Henry Harrison was plagued with requests from artists to sit for them. Since he found posing irksome, he usually refused. One exception was the painter of this portrait, Albert Hoit, who came to Harrison with so many letters of introduction from influential people that Harrison could not refuse. When, early in 1841, the finished portrait went on view at a Boston exhibition, the artist was undoubtedly pleased when a newspaper urged "all good Whigs" to take special notice in the show "of General Harrison by Hoit," which, it claimed, was "one of the best likenesses ever taken" of the subject.

The log cabin and banner above were used in William Henry Harrison's 1840 election campaign. He won by asserting that he was the candidate closest to the people. The Whigs, Harrison's party, cleverly turned the derogatory Democratic remark that if Harrison were given "a barrel of Hard Cider and . . . a pension . . ." he would be content to "sit the remainder of his days in his Log Cabin . . ." into the theme of a populist campaign which recast the wealthy Ohio farmer as a simple backwoodsman.

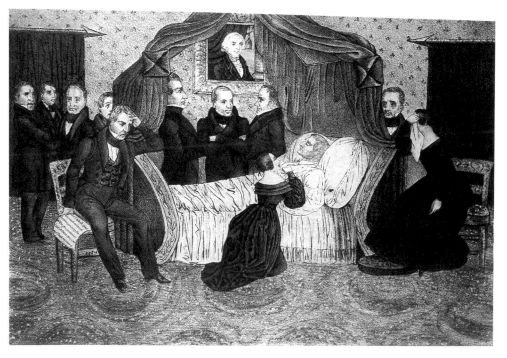

The lithograph at left by Henry R. Robinson depicts the death of William Henry Harrison, the first president to die in office. As a man already of advanced years—he was sixty-eight years old when he was inaugurated as president—the new responsibilities of office tired him even more; he caught a cold in late March which then developed into pneumonia. On April 4, 1841, one month after his inauguration, he was dead.

As a United States senator and the leader of the anti-Jackson coalition that emerged as the Whig party in the early 1830s, Henry Clay wielded great influence over the politics of his day. But he was never quite satisfied. More than anything else he wanted to be president and, for many years, it was clear that should his Whig allies want to make him their White House candidate, he was definitely "available." On three occasions—in 1824, 1832, and 1844—they were inclined to do just that. But in 1840, the year when the Whigs were almost certain to oust the beleaguered Democratic incumbent, Martin Van Buren, they were not. When Clay heard of this, he exploded, "My friends are not worth the powder and shot it would take to kill them."

Instead the Whigs chose as their standard-bearer William Henry Harrison, the sixty-eight-year-old former governor of the Indiana Territory, who had served two undistinguished terms in Congress and had briefly been America's minister to Colombia. Although Harrison's political experience was unimpressive, especially when compared with Clay's, he had one asset that Clay did not. He was a genuine military hero. In the public mind, his victory against the Indians in 1811 at the Battle of Tippecanoe and his defeat of the British during the War of 1812 at the Battle of the Thames were among the country's great moments of martial glory. In short, the Whigs had learned a valuable lesson from their old antagonist Andrew Jackson, who had owed his presidential victory of 1828 largely to his military record. And the lesson was simple: If the choice of presidential nominee is between a well-seasoned politician and a distinguished soldier, support the man with the gold braid and epaulettes.

From Jackson the Whigs had also learned the importance of identifying their candidate with the common man. Consequently, in 1840, Harrison's campaign became a carnival of banner-waving in which his supporters portrayed him as a man who liked to sit outside his humble log cabin chatting with a neighbor over a cup of hard cider. Harrison was not the homespun rustic he was touted as. On the contrary, he came from a patrician family, was the son of a signer of the Declaration of Independence, and had been raised in an elegant plantation mansion in Virginia. In addition, his Ohio home was a far cry from the simple one-room cabin that Whig propaganda implied. The truth, however, remained irrelevant in the campaign. While Harrison was discreetly silent about any real political issues, a majority of the electorate soon became convinced that "Old Tippecanoe" was their man.

Unfortunately, it will never be known how effective a president Harrison would have been. Within a month of delivering the longest inaugural address ever, he contracted pneumonia and died. Nevertheless, it is possible to surmise what his presidency might have been. Judging, for example, from his several months as president-elect when Harrison promised the same posts to two or three office-seekers, his administration might well have been best remembered for its chaos. Either that, or a group of powerful Whigs—among them Henry Clay—might have taken him firmly in hand and made themselves the power behind the throne.

BORN
Berkeley, Charles City County, Virginia, February 9, 1773

ANCESTRY
English

WIFE
Anna Tuthill Symmes
Born: Morristown, New Jersey
July 25, 1775
Died: North Bend, Ohio
February 25, 1864

MARRIED
North Bend, Ohio, November 25, 1795

CHILDREN
Elizabeth Bassett (1796-1846)   Benjamin (1806-1840)
John Symmes (1798-1830)   Mary Symmes (1809-1842)
Lucy Singleton (1800-1826)   Carter Bassett (1811-1839)
William Henry (1802-1838)   Anna Tuthill (1813-1845)
John Scott (1804-1878)   James Findlay (1814-1817)

HOME
Grouseland, Vincennes, Indiana

EDUCATION
Attended Hampden-Sydney College, Hampden-Sydney, Virginia
(1790)
Studied medicine with Benjamin Rush in Philadelphia, Pennsylvania (1791)

RELIGION
Episcopalian

OCCUPATIONS
Soldier and politician

MILITARY SERVICE
Rose from ensign to captain, U.S. Army (1791-1798)
Governor of Indiana Territory, fought Indians at Tippecanoe (1811)
Commissioned major general of Kentucky militia (1812)
Rose from brigadier general to major general in command of Northwest Territory, U.S. Army (1812-1814)

PREPRESIDENTIAL OFFICES
Secretary of the Northwest Territory (1798-1799)
U.S. representative from the Northwest Territory (1799-1800)
Governor of Indiana Territory and Superindendent of Indian Affairs (1801-1813)
Member of the U.S. House of Representatives (1816-1819)
Member of the Ohio State Senate (1819-1821)
Member of the U.S. Senate (1825-1828)
Minister to Colombia (1828-1829)

POLITICAL PARTY
Whig

INAUGURATED AS PRESIDENT
March 4, 1841, the Capitol, Washington, D.C.

AGE AT INAUGURATION
68

DIED
Washington, D.C., April 4, 1841, age 68

JOHN TYLER

TENTH PRESIDENT   1841–1845

The creator of John Tyler's portrait, George P. A. Healy, was among the most sought-after portraitists in the pre-Civil War United States. The list of his subjects reads like a Who's Who of his day, and Tyler sat for two likenesses by him—once in the White House and again at Tyler's Virginia plantation in 1859. This picture dates from the later sitting. Although Tyler was nearing seventy when he posed for it, some of the dogged stubbornness that had made him the bane of fellow Whigs in the 1840s still remained, and a hint of that quality seems to be apparent in the portrait.

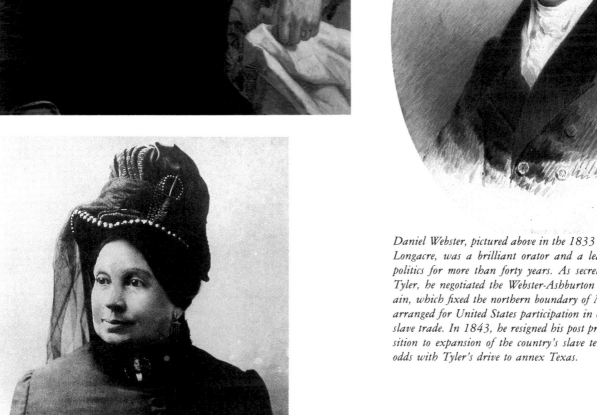

Daniel Webster, pictured above in the 1833 portrait by James Barton Longacre, was a brilliant orator and a leading figure in national politics for more than forty years. As secretary of state under John Tyler, he negotiated the Webster-Ashburton Treaty with Great Britain, which fixed the northern boundary of Maine with Canada and arranged for United States participation in efforts to stop the African slave trade. In 1843, he resigned his post primarily because his opposition to expansion of the country's slave territories had put him at odds with Tyler's drive to annex Texas.

Julia Gardiner married John Tyler in 1844, two years after the death of his first wife Letitia. She was wealthy and vivacious, and, at twenty-four, thirty years younger than her husband. She brightened the last year of his presidency and was credited by Tyler with playing an important role in promoting the annexation of Texas. This photograph was taken later in her life.

During the presidential campaign of 1840, the most often heard cry was "Tippecanoe and Tyler Too." In rallying to that Whig party slogan, voters had their eyes fixed on the man referred to in the first word of that phrase, White House hopeful William Henry Harrison, whose army had triumphed over the Shawnee Indians in the Battle of Tippecanoe in 1811. For most, his vice-presidential running mate, John Tyler, represented no more than a catchy poetical afterthought. But the electorate that ultimately swept Harrison into the presidency would have done well to consider Tyler a bit more carefully. Just a month after Harrison's inauguration, Tyler became the first vice-president to succeed to the nation's highest office due to the death of the president.

Formerly a states' rights Democrat who had switched his political loyalties because of dissatisfaction with Andrew Jackson's assertive administration, Tyler was never fully at ease with the Whig eagerness to expand the federal government's role in American life. Consequently, shortly after assuming the presidency, he found himself at bitter odds with his fellow Whigs in Congress over the legislative attempt to reestablish a national bank. When he refused to sign a bill authorizing that institution, most of his cabinet resigned in protest, and he became an outcast in his own party. Throughout the rest of his presidency, Whig publicists vied to outdo each other in vilifying this "reptilelike" man who had accidently made his way into the White House.

Despite stormy relations with fellow Whigs, both in and out of Congress, Tyler's administration was not without its accomplishments. By the time he retired to his Virginia plantation in 1845, he could lay claim to settling the Canada-Maine boundary dispute that had plagued Anglo-American relations for years. He could also take a large share of the credit for the annexation of Texas.

Perhaps Tyler's most important legacy, however, was the precedent he set as the country's first unelected president. In taking office at Harrison's death, he had not, as some thought he should, acted merely as a caretaker, subservient to the wishes of his Harrison-appointed cabinet advisers and their congressional allies. Rather he had assumed the presidential powers in his own right. In so doing, he incurred great unpopularity in many quarters, but he also provided a valuable example for future vice-presidents who found themselves in the same situation.

For the next fifteen years, Tyler lived in relative obscurity. On the eve of the Civil War, however, hoping to prevent an armed conflict, he reentered the public arena to preside over the Washington Peace Convention. When the convention failed to achieve sectional peace, he joined his fortunes to the southern Confederacy. Shortly before his death, Tyler was elected to the Confederate House of Representatives. Thus, the first vice-president to succeed to the presidency as a result of an incumbent's death also became the only former president to turn actively against the Union he had once led.

John Tyler

BORN
Charles City County, Virginia, March 29, 1790

ANCESTRY
English

FIRST WIFE	SECOND WIFE
Letitia Christian	Julia Gardiner
Born:	Born:
New Kent County, Virginia	Gardiner's Island, New York
November 12, 1790	May 4, 1820
Died: Washington, D.C.	Died:
September 10, 1842	Richmond, Virginia July 10, 1889

MARRIED
First wife:
New Kent County, Virginia, March 29, 1813
Second Wife:
New York, N.Y., June 26, 1844

CHILDREN

By first wife:	By second wife:
Mary (1815-1848)	David Gardiner (1846-1927)
Robert (1816-1877)	John Alexander (1848-1883)
John (1819-1896)	Julia (1849-1871)
Letitia (1821-1907)	Lachlan (1851-1902)
Elizabeth (1823-1850)	Lyon Gardiner (1853-1935)
Alice (1827-1854)	Robert Fitzwalter (1856-1927)
Tazewell (1830-1874)	Pearl (1860-1947)

HOME
Sherwood Forest, Charles City County, Virginia

EDUCATION
Attended College of William and Mary, Williamsburg, Virginia (1807)
Studied law with father (1807-1809)

RELIGION
Episcopalian

OCCUPATIONS
Lawyer

MILITARY SERVICE
Captain of Volunteer Company in Richmond, Virginia (1813)

PREPRESIDENTIAL OFFICES
Member of the Virginia House of Delegates
(1811-1815 and 1823-1825)
Member of the U.S. House of Representatives (1816-1821)
Governor of Virginia (1825-1827)
Member of the U.S. Senate (1827-1836)
Vice-President (1841)

POLITICAL PARTY
Whig

INAUGURATED AS PRESIDENT
April 6, 1841, Indian Queen Hotel, Washington, D.C.

AGE AT INAUGURATION
51

DIED
Richmond, Virginia, January 18, 1862, age 71

JAMES K. POLK

ELEVENTH PRESIDENT   1845–1849

The Calvinistic James K. Polk had nothing but disdain for "time unprofitably spent." He once boasted that he was the "hardest-working man in this country." This did not mean, however, that he never had time for lighter pursuits. When the painter Miner Kellogg came to Washington in 1848, Polk not only agreed to pose for this portrait, he also took time out from his presidential duties to accompany Kellogg to an exhibition featuring Hiram Powers's internationally acclaimed sculpture, entitled The Greek Slave.

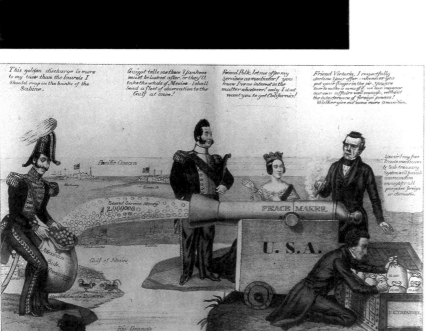

As this cartoon indicates, before resorting to war to gain his ambitious territorial aims in the Southwest, Polk empowered an emissary to offer Mexico money in return for the cession of a region that included California, New Mexico, and Arizona. Meanwhile, Britain and France (represented in the cartoon by Queen Victoria and King Louis Philippe) maneuvered to thwart Polk's goal. Neither the American offer nor the Anglo-French scheming, however, had much effect and Polk had to achieve his territorial goals through war, but he did achieve them.

Many Whigs were greatly cheered in the presidential contest of 1844 when they learned that Henry Clay, their White House hopeful, would be running against James K. Polk, the relatively unknown dark-horse Democrat. In light of Clay's thirty years of national prominence and distinction as a skillful conciliator of the country's sectional differences, they reasoned, he would have little trouble beating Polk at the polls. But Clay knew better. Upon being told that Polk was to oppose him in his third try for the presidency, he groaned, "Beaten again, by God." Actually, Clay's defeat was largely his own fault. While he tried to placate both North and South by waffling on the issue of annexing the slaveholding territory of Texas, Polk —on the advice of former President Andrew Jackson— forthrightly championed the acquisition of that territory. He read the nation's expansionist mood more accurately than Clay and by a narrow margin defeated him.

In selecting a standard-bearer for the presidential campaign of 1844, the Democrats had a number of choices well known to the nation's electorate, not least of whom was former president Martin Van Buren. But in the end, they bypassed this front-running contender for their party's endorsement, as well as a number of other logical possibilities. Instead, they added to the country's fund of minor political lore by entering in the White House sweepstakes James K. Polk, the first "dark horse" candidate in the nation's history. Consequently, the favorite remark among the Democrats' Whig opposition in 1844 took the form of the belittling question, "Who is James K. Polk?"

Polk was not quite as obscure as that inquiry suggests. During his tenure in the House of Representatives from 1825 to 1839, he had exercised considerable influence and had been one of the Jackson administration's most potent congressional allies. During his last four years, as House Speaker, he had also revealed remarkable gifts for bringing even the most obstreperous politicians to his parliamentarian's heel.

Nevertheless, it was not Polk's congressional record that explained his presidential nomination and ultimate victory at the polls. Rather it was his frankly stated view that there should be an aggressive policy to promote America's westward expansion. With expansionist sentiment running at full tide in 1844, such an attitude was the very thing needed to spur Polk from his dark horse starting position and through the White House door.

Polk embarked on his presidency with four objectives: He wanted Congress to lower the country's tariffs; he wished to acquire California from Mexico; he wanted to settle the Anglo-American dispute over the Canada-Oregon boundary; and he intended to reestablish Martin Van Buren's Independent Treasury System, which had been abolished in 1841. Because he achieved all these goals in only four years, Polk is often counted among the country's most effective presidents.

At least one of these accomplishments—the acquisition of California—was not realized, however, without great costs. When Mexico turned down his administration's offer to purchase California, Polk decided that his only alternative was to provoke a war with that country. Although the subsequent conflict had popular support, many objected strenuously to his resort to arms for a territory that rightfully belonged to another country. More serious, however, was the suspicion, voiced by Polk's critics, that sowed some of the earliest seeds of the Civil War. The hostilities with Mexico, they charged, were being waged to facilitate the South's expansion of its slaveholding empire. When the Mexican War ended in 1848 with the annexation of both California and the New Mexico Territory, that suspicion grew into a certainty as the North and South opened their bitter debate about whether these new territories should be slave or free.

The success of Polk's administration also exacted great personal costs. A secretive man who insisted on controlling every phase of his presidency, Polk was incapable of delegating responsibility. For him this was a source of pride. But the long hours devoted to the affairs of state took a tremendous toll on Polk's health, which was not good to begin with. Within four months of leaving the White House he was dead.

BORN
Mecklenburg County, North Carolina
November 2, 1795

ANCESTRY
Scottish-Irish

WIFE
Sarah Childress
Born: Murfreesboro, Tennessee
September 4, 1803
Died: Nashville, Tennessee
August 14, 1891

MARRIED
Murfreesboro, Tennessee, January 1, 1824

CHILDREN
None

HOME
Polk House, Columbia, Tennessee

EDUCATION
University of North Carolina, Chapel Hill, North Carolina;
B.A. (1818)

RELIGION
Presbyterian

OCCUPATION
Lawyer

PREPRESIDENTIAL OFFICES
Member of the Tennessee Legislature (1823-1825)
Member of the U.S. House of Representatives (1825-1839)
Speaker of the House of Representatives (1835-1839)
Governor of Tennessee (1839-1841)

POLITICAL PARTY
Democratic

INAUGURATED AS PRESIDENT
March 4, 1845, the Capitol, Washington D.C.

AGE AT INAUGURATION
49

DIED
Nashville, Tennessee, June 15, 1849, age 53

ZACHARY TAYLOR

TWELFTH PRESIDENT   1849–1850

This portrait of Zachary Taylor, dating from the year of his election, depicts him in a more sedate and decorous light than the reality of his appearance often warranted. Whether in or out of uniform, Taylor generally did not much bother about his attire. What struck many contemporaries most when they first saw him was the air of casual shabbiness that he conveyed, with his frayed jackets and his wrinkled pants stuffed carelessly into well-worn boots.

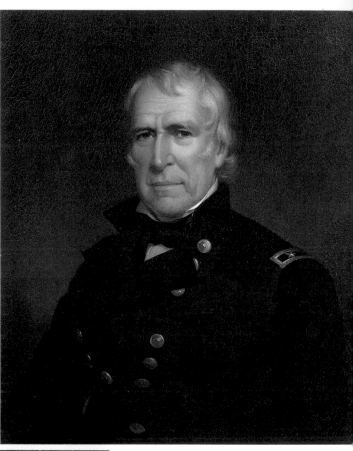

Zachary Taylor's exploits during the Mexican War made him a national military hero and enormously popular with the American public. During the presidential campaign of 1848, his likeness adorned even such everyday objects as the mirror above. When Taylor was inaugurated as president in 1849, he was greeted by the largest crowd the capital had ever seen; when he died sixteen months later, his body was followed to the gravesite by a funeral procession about two miles long with thousands of mourners lining the route.

Painted during the Mexican War at one of Zachary Taylor's military encampments, this picture was the work of William Garl Brown who had been sent by a Whig newspaper editor in Virginia to paint a portrait of Taylor to be used in promoting the General's presidential candidacy of 1848. Brown ultimately exceeded his client's request and produced several images. In the scene here, Taylor is shown with members of his staff. To the left is his horse, Whitey, who, in the course of Taylor's great victories over the Mexican army, became almost as famous as his owner.

President James K. Polk's war with Mexico achieved his territorial aims. But even as those aims were being reached, Polk sensed that built into this military triumph was trouble for his own Democratic party. For out of the war there had come a new hero whose charisma threatened to earn him the Whig nomination in the presidential election of 1848. Polk knew that if that happened, his party would have all it could do to hold on to the White House.

The name of this threat to the Democrats was Zachary Taylor, the leathery-faced "rough and ready" general who had defeated the Mexican armies at the battles of Palo Alto, Monterrey, and Buena Vista. When reports of his martial prowess began reaching the eastern seaboard in 1846, many Whigs realized that he personified a golden opportunity. Not only was Taylor a national hero; his homespun appearance and well-known indifference to rules of military protocol were assets that were certain to play well among the voters. There was only one problem: No one was certain whether the apolitical Taylor, who had never voted in a presidential election, would consent to run.

When first asked about this possibility, Taylor unequivocally declared that even if victory at the polls were assured, "I would not be a candidate." But his Whig supporters did not believe him, and in the face of further courting, "Old Rough and Ready's" once flat denial of any presidential ambition began to take on a decidedly more qualified edge. So, with the door to Taylor's candidacy ajar, the campaign to send him to the White House was on. But in one respect the hero of Buena Vista remained apolitical to the end: When the final vote count proclaimed him the winner, he could claim the singular distinction of becoming president without bothering to cast his own vote.

At his inaugural ceremonies, Taylor stated that the main object of his administration was to "harmonize conflicting interests, and . . . perpetuate the Union." But with the nation locked in angry debate about a number of issues related to slavery, including its extension to the newly acquired California and New Mexico territories, that proved a difficult goal to achieve.

Though a southern slaveholder himself, Taylor feared the North's deepening animosity toward slavery, and he considered its spread a dangerous threat to the nation's unity. As a result, he was firmly determined to thwart the South's drive to permit slavery in either California or New Mexico and to oppose demands from the slaveholding state of Texas that part of New Mexico be ceded to it. This unwillingness to give the South any quarter, however, only fueled the fires of disunity further. By mid-1850, Taylor's opposition to Congress's compromise plan, granting various concessions to the South's slave interests, seemed to be pushing the country toward civil war. But the sudden death of Taylor changed everything. With Vice-President Millard Fillmore now in the White House, Congress was able to enact its compromise without fear of a presidential veto, and the unity that Taylor had promised at his inauguration was restored, at least for the moment.

BORN
Montebello, Orange County, Virginia, November 24, 1784

ANCESTRY
English

WIFE
Margaret Mackall Smith
Born: Calvert, County, Maryland
September 21, 1788
Died: Pascagoula, Mississippi
August 18, 1852

MARRIED
Jefferson County, Kentucky, June 21, 1810

CHILDREN
Anne Mackall (1811-1875)
Sarah Knox (1814-1835)
Octavia Pannill (1816-1820)
Margaret Smith (1819-1820)
Mary Elizabeth (1824-1909)
Richard (1826-1879)

EDUCATION
No formal education

RELIGION
Episcopalian

OCCUPATIONS
Soldier and farmer

MILITARY SERVICE
Volunteer in Kentucky militia (1803)
Rose from first lieutenant to major general, U.S. Army
(1808-1849)

POLITICAL PARTY
Whig

INAUGURATED AS PRESIDENT
March 5, 1849, the Capitol, Washington, D.C.

AGE AT INAUGURATION
64

DIED
Washington, D.C., July 9, 1850, age 65

MILLARD FILLMORE

THIRTEENTH PRESIDENT   1850–1853

Millard Fillmore's portrait by an unidentified artist is believed to date from about the time he retired from Congress in the early 1840s. During his ten years in the House of Representatives, the hulking and amiable Fillmore had become a substantial and widely respected influence. But when he left the House he was less interested in holding on to that influence than he was in returning to his native New York to reconcile some of the differences that were dividing his Whig party there.

Although poor health forced Abigail Powers Fillmore to delegate many of her responsibilities as First Lady to her daughter, she was able to secure from Congress an appropriation to establish a library in the White House.

In this engraving, Fillmore can been seen on the left fulfilling his vice-presidential responsibilities as presiding officer of the Senate while Henry Clay presents his Compromise of 1850, which was designed to quell national disharmony over slavery. In the days following Clay's speech, Fillmore worried that he might be called upon to cast the deciding vote on some of the proposals. If that happened, his desire for peace dictated that, although he considered slavery wrong, he would vote for the Compromise including those sections of it that promoted southern slave interests. But that would have meant defying President Zachary Taylor's rigid opposition to the Compromise's concessions to slavery. Taylor's death saved Fillmore from having to oppose openly the man whose adminstration he served.

Tall and husky, good-natured and outgoing, Millard Fillmore was a one-time member of the House of Representatives and Zachary Taylor's vice-president. He entered the White House after Taylor died in office in 1850. A man of principle and strong conviction, Fillmore could claim credit for dispatching Commodore Matthew Perry on his successful mission to convince Japan to end its centuries of isolation by opening its ports to American shipping and commerce. It was Fillmore, too, who had blocked France's Napoleon III from claiming dominion over Hawaii and who thwarted southern conspiracies to annex Spanish-held Cuba to the United States.

Fillmore's greatest distinction, however, grew out of his role in averting the very real possibility of civil war in 1850. Unlike Taylor, who had balked at the Congress's compromise measures for placating both North and South in the debate over the expansion of slavery, Fillmore believed in compromise. Consequently, it was his succession to the presidency that finally permitted the five bills of the Great Compromise to pass through Congress without the threat of a White House veto.

Some historians fault Fillmore for this, claiming that his signing of the compromise bills only delayed the inevitable armed confrontation between North and South, which, had it taken place in 1850, would have been far less costly. Although that charge might seem a bit harsh, it is nevertheless true that, like many well-meaning politicians of his day, Fillmore failed to understand that his country had passed the point where compromise on the slavery issue was possible.

Thus, Fillmore's signatures on the bills that made up the Compromise of 1850 were barely dry before it was apparent that the resulting tranquility in the nation was temporary at best. The most dramatic indication of that lamentable fact was northern anger over one of the Compromise's major concessions to the South, a new law promising strong federal support in the capture of runaway slaves. When Fillmore made clear that despite his own aversion to slavery, he meant to enforce the Fugitive Slave Act to the letter, this anger soon translated into action. While armed Bostonians sought to prevent the apprehension of alleged runaways in their city, Harriet Beecher Stowe expressed her indignation by writing that most persuasive antislavery tract, *Uncle Tom's Cabin.* Meanwhile, across the North the ranks of committed abolitionists began to swell as they never had before. And, as the South watched those events transpire, its hostility for the North deepened yet further.

Simply put, Fillmore's facilitation of the Compromise of 1850 produced mixed results. On the one hand, it momentarily eased sectional tensions. On the other, it added new sources of friction between North and South and, in so doing, moved the country one step closer to the very war that Fillmore had hoped to prevent.

BORN
Summerhill, Cayuga County, New York, January 7, 1800

ANCESTRY
English

FIRST WIFE
Abigail Powers
Born: Stillwater, New York
March 13, 1798
Died: Washington, D.C.
March 30, 1853

SECOND WIFE
Caroline Carmichael McIntosh
Born: Morristown, New Jersey
October 21, 1813
Died: Buffalo, New York
August 11, 1881

MARRIED
First wife: Moravia, New York, February 5, 1826
Second wife: Albany, New York, February 10, 1858

CHILDREN
By first wife:
Millard Powers (1828-1889)
Mary Abigail (1832-1854)

EDUCATION
Studied law in Cayuga County and Buffalo, New York

RELIGION
Unitarian

OCCUPATIONS
Lawyer, politician, and chancellor of the
University of Buffalo

PREPRESIDENTIAL OFFICES
Member of the New York Legislature (1829-1831)
Member of the U.S. House of Representatives
(1833-1835 and 1837-1843)
New York State Comptroller (1848-1849)
Vice-President (1849-1850)

POLITICAL PARTY
Whig during Presidency
American from 1854

INAUGURATED AS PRESIDENT
July 10, 1850, Hall of the House of Representatives,
Washington, D.C.

AGE AT INAUGURATION
50

DIED
Buffalo, New York, March 8, 1874, age 74

FRANKLIN PIERCE

FOURTEENTH PRESIDENT   1853–1857

As this portrait dating from the first year of Franklin Pierce's presidency indicates, Pierce may well have been the handsomest man ever to sit in the White House. But, of course, good looks were not enough. Even before Pierce took office, one contemporary noted, many of those who supported him during the campaign of 1852 were becoming decidedly uneasy about his adequacy for the job.

The print above, captioned "Southern Chivalry—Argument versus Club's," shows southern Representative Preston Brooks savagely beating the abolitionist Senator Charles Sumner because of the vehement speech he had made denouncing the Kansas-Nebraska Act, which opened the two territories to slavery. Franklin Pierce signed the bill into law in 1854, believing it would ensure him southern Democratic support in the future. Instead, it resulted in his political destruction and a bloody guerilla war in Kansas between pro- and anti-slave settlers.

One of the few successes of Pierce's administration was a treaty negotiated in 1854 that opened isolationist Japan to American trade. But even this was more to the credit of his White House predecessor, Millard Fillmore, who two years earlier had sent Commodore Matthew Perry to Japan to make the agreement. This lithograph depicts Perry's landing at Shimoda, Japan, in June 1854.

When Nathaniel Hawthorne agreed to help promote the presidential candidacy of his old college friend Franklin Pierce by writing Pierce's biography, he found himself somewhat hard-pressed for material. Indeed, Pierce's rise from a seat in the New Hampshire legislature to membership in the House of Representatives and, finally, the Senate, was decidedly lacking in both distinction and drama. To make matters worse, the story behind his presidential nomination by the Democrats did not promise a campaign that would present Pierce in a flattering light. For he owed his Democratic nomination not to his proven ability, but rather to his reputation as a northerner with southern sympathy, who, in that election year torn by the continuing debate over slavery, seemed eminently "safe." Good material or not, Hawthorne was determined not to let his friend down and did produce a biography that was moderately engaging. But as Hawthorne himself observed, "it took a romancer" to make it so.

Like his predecessor Millard Fillmore, Pierce entered the White House intent on maintaining a peaceful equilibrium between the increasingly abolitionist North and the slaveholding South. There were two factors that made this especially difficult. First, just before his inauguration, Pierce had witnessed the death of his eleven-year-old son in a train accident. Consequently, he took up his presidential duties in an emotionally distraught state. Second, he was never a particularly strong personality, and his desire to please everyone made him all too susceptible to injudicious advice.

Thus, Pierce allowed some of his southern-oriented advisers to drag his administration into an aborted conspiracy to wrest from Spain the island of Cuba, which the South had long considered a likely place for expansion of its slave interests. He also listened sympathetically to railroad promoters anxious to build a transcontinental line across the Great Plains to the Pacific. This was admirable, except for one of the enterprise's requirements. Before it could be launched, it was necessary to establish territorial governments for the regions of Kansas and Nebraska. To gain southern congressional support for that action, the Kansas-Nebraska Act signed into law by Pierce in 1854 contained a proviso opening up these lands, previously closed to slavery, to settlement by southern slaveholders.

The consequences of this catering to southern interests were disastrous for the nation and for Pierce. Soon after the Kansas-Nebraska Act took effect, Kansas became a bloody battleground with pro-slavery and abolitionist settlers pledging themselves to fight for control of the region literally to the death. As for Pierce, a good many of his fellow northerners could not find words harsh enough to describe this man who seemed to be selling out to the South's rapacious demands.

While Ralph Waldo Emerson speculated that the only excuse for Pierce's politics was "imbecility," others characterized him and his advisers as the "tools and lickspittles" of the slave power. But, worst of all, Pierce had helped to raise northern antislavery sentiment to near fever pitch and in the process made future accommodations between North and South almost impossible to achieve.

BORN
Hillsboro, New Hampshire, November 23, 1804

ANCESTRY
English

WIFE
Jane Means Appleton
Born: Hampton, New Hampshire
March 12, 1806
Died: Andover, Massachusetts
December 2, 1863

MARRIED
Amherst, New Hampshire, November 19, 1834

CHILDREN
Frank Robert (1839-1843)
Benjamin (1841-1853)

HOME
Pierce Homestead, Hillsboro Upper Village,
New Hampshire

EDUCATION
Bowdoin College, Brunswick, Maine; B.A. (1824)
Studied law with Levi Woodbury, Portsmouth, New
Hampshire (1825)

RELIGION
Episcopalian

OCCUPATIONS
Lawyer, politician, and soldier

MILITARY SERVICE
Brigadier general, U.S. Army (1847-1848)

PREPRESIDENTIAL OFFICES
Member and Speaker of the New Hampshire Legislature
(1829-1833)
Member of the U.S. House of Representatives (1833-1837)
Member of the U.S. Senate (1837-1842)
President of the New Hampshire Constitutional Convention
(1850)

POLITICAL PARTY
Democratic

INAUGURATED AS PRESIDENT
March 4, 1853, the Capitol, Washington, D.C.

AGE AT INAUGURATION
48

DIED
Concord, New Hampshire, October 8, 1869, age 64

JAMES BUCHANAN

FIFTEENTH PRESIDENT   1857–1861

When the southern secession crisis led to the outbreak of the Civil War shortly after James Buchanan left office in 1861, many placed the blame squarely on Buchanan's shoulders, and he soon became the object of considerable hatred and petty slights. A good example was the original version of this portrait by G. P. A. Healy, which had been intended for the federal government. When the time came, in 1861, to pay for the painting, Congress was in no mood to allocate funds for a picture of the man who had, it claimed, let the South secede without lifting a finger. In using this rationale to deny payment for the portrait, however, the members of the Congress failed to remember that they themselves had hampered Buchanan from blocking secession by ignoring his requests for authorization to act.

James Buchanan was a northern Democrat who was sympathetic to the South and preached compromise on the slavery issue. His insistence that abolitionists should show restraint and tolerance resulted in the strong southern support which won him the presidency. At left is a ribbon from Buchanan's 1856 presidential campaign. The rooster was at that time the Democratic Party symbol.

In 1859, abolitionist John Brown, left, led an unsuccessful raid on the arsenal at Harper's Ferry, Virginia, in an attempt to start a slave rebellion. Brown was captured, brought to trial, and hung. To southern slave owners he symbolized the very real and fearful possibility of a violent overthrow of their way of life. To northern abolitionists he became a martyr to a noble cause.

Following John Brown's slave-freeing raid of 1859, Buchanan sent federal agents in search of Frederick Douglass, the former slave and noted abolitionist, right, in the belief that he had aided Brown. Although Douglass had tried to discourage Brown, he did not want to risk explanations to government officials and decided to seek refuge in England.

In opening up the Kansas Territory to slavery, the Kansas-Nebraska Act of 1854 caused angry feelings of betrayal in the North, the intensity of which had never before been felt in the nation's seething debate over slavery. In the wake of that anger, a new political party had arisen, dedicated to halting the spread of slavery. By 1856, this fledgling coalition, known as the Republicans, was fielding western explorer John C. Fremont as its first presidential candidate. Most of the electorate of both North and South, however, still hoped that the growing rift between them could be settled peaceably. As a result, fearing that Republican militance would force a final rupturing of the Union, the voters of 1856 rejected Fremont in favor of the Democratic candidate, James Buchanan.

Judging from Buchanan's record, the decision was a wise one, and his frank confession that he deplored slavery while recognizing a constitutional necessity to protect it made him seem like the embodiment of evenhandedness needed to cool the nation's temper. Even more reassuring, in his forty years of public life, he proved that he had the ability to make his way unscathed through the labyrinths of political divisiveness.

Unfortunately, the task of curbing the growing volatility of the slavery issue was beyond the capacities of even this astute politician. Indeed, Buchanan's attempts to promote harmony only drove the North and South farther apart. When, for example, the strife-torn Kansas Territory came under the control of its pro-slavery factions and applied to Congress for admission to the Union as a slave state, Buchanan felt compelled to support this action. In the process, of course, the abolitionist temper in the North waxed more militant than ever. Also feeding this militance was the Supreme Court decision of 1857 in *Dred Scott* v. *Sanford,* which focused on the question of whether extended residence in a territory where Congress had prohibited slavery made the slave Dred Scott free. With pressuring from Buchanan to settle definitively the long-festering debate over slaveholders' rights in congressionally controlled areas, the court declared that Congress had no power to ban slavery. With that, many in the abolitionist movement became convinced that nothing short of war could keep the blot of slavery from spreading. And a war, of a kind at least, was exactly what "Bleeding Kansas" and the Dred Scott case precipitated. In 1859, a band of armed men led by John Brown launched their abortive slave-freeing raid into Virginia.

Now it was the South's turn to be wildly indignant. As Buchanan moved into his final year in the White House, his hopes of pacifying North and South were shattered. Much worse, however, lay ahead. When Abraham Lincoln, the anti-slavery Republican candidate, claimed victory in the presidential election of 1860, southerners believed that they had no alternative but to leave the Union. One southern state after another acted on that conviction and during his last months in office, Buchanan found himself presiding over the worst crisis since the Revolution. But, as a lame duck president, he was powerless to deal with it.

It was hardly surprising that in March 1861 Buchanan turned over the White House to Lincoln with a sigh of relief. "If you are as happy on entering . . . this house as I am in leaving it," he told his successor, "you are the happiest man in the country."

BORN
Cove Gap, Pennsylvania, April 23, 1791

ANCESTRY
Scottish-Irish

MARRIED
Never married

HOME
Wheatland, Lancaster, Pennsylvania

EDUCATION
Dickinson College, Carlisle, Pennsylvania; B.A. (1809)
Studied law with James Hopkins, Lancaster, Pennsylvania
(1809)

RELIGION
Presbyterian

OCCUPATION
Lawyer

PREPRESIDENTIAL OFFICES
Member of the Pennsylvania Legislature (1814-1816)
Member of the U.S. House of Representatives (1821-1831)
Minister to Russia (1832-1833)
Member of the U.S. Senate (1834-1845)
Secretary of State (1845-1849)
Minister to Great Britain (1853-1856)

POLITICAL PARTY
Federalist then Democratic

INAUGURATED AS PRESIDENT
March 4, 1857, the Capitol, Washington, D.C.

AGE AT INAUGURATION
65

DIED
Lancaster, Pennsylvania, June 1, 1868, age 77

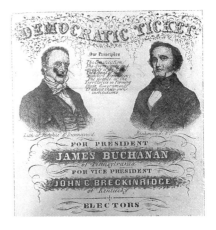

ABRAHAM LINCOLN

SIXTEENTH PRESIDENT 1861–1865

In the presidential campaign of 1860, Abraham Lincoln's supporters had a hard time coming to terms with his raw, homely face, and when commissioning a campaign portrait of him, one of them actually told the artist to make the likeness "good looking whether the original justify it or not." By the end of his presidency, however, Lincoln's features had softened. That, combined with his growing reputation as emancipator of the slaves and savior of the Union, made such instructions unnecessary. When G. P. A. Healy went to the White House in 1864 to do the preliminary drawings for this portrait, he needed no prompting to cast Lincoln in a flattering, romantic light.

The assassination of Abraham Lincoln stunned and saddened the nation. Doorways were covered in crepe and men and women wept for the man who had led them through the four devastating and crippling years of the Civil War. Tens of thousands of mourners viewed the body as it lay in state and later when it was transported back by train to his home state on the same route the President had taken to his inauguration in Washington. Lincoln's body was laid to rest on May 4, 1865, at Oak Ridge Cemetery in Springfield, Ohio. Shown above is the bugle used to blow final taps at the funeral.

Pictured below are President Lincoln and his cabinet at the first reading of the 1862 Emancipation Proclamation. To the great dissatisfaction of abolitionists, it freed slaves only in states under Confederate domination and not in areas controlled by the Union.

In the campaign of 1860, Lincoln's Republican supporters often played down their party's anti-slavery position to appeal to the more moderate-minded electorate. Instead they emphasized Lincoln's humble origins, and, as this campaign banner shows, they anointed him the "Prince of Rails"—a title inspired by his early days as a frontier log splitter.

In any opinion poll asking Americans whom they consider to be their greatest presidents, it is a certainty that George Washington and Abraham Lincoln would top the list. It is, therefore, one of the more intriguing ironies of presidential campaign history that while Washington won the nation's highest office by virtually unanimous popular consent, Lincoln claimed it by garnering less than 40 percent of the votes. Thus, it can hardly be said that Lincoln's elevation to the presidency in 1860 resulted from a widely held perception that he was the proverbial "right man for the moment." Rather, he owed his success in the election to the nation's slavery crisis, which had thrown his opposition into disarray, and instead of facing one candidate in the campaign, he faced three. As a result, although the final ballot count indicated that a solid majority of the electorate disliked Lincoln and his abolitionist Republican party, they had sufficiently divided their votes among his three opponents to make him the victor.

In contrast to Washington, then, whose presidential merits seemed obvious even before he took office, Lincoln faced a steep climb before he would reach his own Olympian heights. In fact, as his election became the final spur in driving the South from the Union and the nation into a bloody civil war, it seemed that this homely, lanky Illinois lawyer was destined for an unexalted place in history.

Mocked and disdained for his earthy humor and rustic appearance, Lincoln was beset from the start by criticism from all sides. On the one hand, his attempt to curb the activities of the North's southern sympathizers through arbitrary arrest and temporary suspension of basic civil rights drew accusations of despotism from his enemies. On the other hand, his initial insistence that his main goal in the Civil War was restoration of the Union and not the wholesale elimination of slavery led to charges of moral cowardice among his more radical abolitionist allies. And when the war went badly for Union forces, particularly at the outset, he was made to take much of the blame.

Although the barrage of criticism never entirely ceased, northern victories on the battlefield at least somewhat blunted it. Still, it was not combat success alone that muffled Lincoln's critics; it was also Lincoln himself. As he brought his unique blend of pragmatic realism, patient forbearance, and compassion to bear on his administration, he gradually assumed a grandeur that was larger than life. Moreover, after it became clear that his Emancipation Proclamation of 1863, calling for the freeing of slaves in territories controlled by the southern armies, was not merely an unenforceable sop to abolitionists but the very real death knell for slavery everywhere, that grandeur began to have an almost saintly aura.

Lincoln's final investiture, however, as one of the country's two unassailably great presidents did not occur until after his death at the hands of a southern assassin in April 1865. In the wake of this martyrdom to his country's cause, the many alleged blemishes of his wartime administration soon disappeared and were replaced by an almost mystical adoration of the "Great Emancipator."

BORN
Hodgenville, Hardin County, Kentucky, February 12, 1809

ANCESTRY
English

WIFE
Mary Todd
Born: Lexington, Kentucky
December 13, 1818
Died: Springfield, Illinois
July 16, 1882

MARRIED
Springfield, Illinois, November 4, 1842

CHILDREN
Robert Todd (1843-1926)
Edward Baker (1846-1850)
William Wallace (1850-1862)
Thomas (Tad) (1853-1871)

HOME
Eighth and Jackson Streets, Springfield, Illinois

EDUCATION
Self-educated

RELIGION
No denomination

OCCUPATIONS
Store clerk, store owner, ferry pilot, surveyor, postmaster, and lawyer

MILITARY SERVICE
Scout in volunteer company for three months during Black Hawk War (1832)

PREPRESIDENTIAL OFFICES
Member of the Illinois General Assembly (1834-1842)
Member of the U.S. House of Representatives (1847-1849)

POLITICAL PARTY
Republican

INAUGURATED AS PRESIDENT
First term: March 4, 1861, the Capitol, Washington, D.C.
Second term: March 4, 1865, the Capitol, Washington, D.C.

AGE AT INAUGURATION
52

DIED
Washington, D.C., April 15, 1865, age 56

ANDREW JOHNSON

SEVENTEENTH PRESIDENT   1865–1869

Whether the Tennessee artist Washington Cooper intended it or not, his somber portrait of Andrew Johnson seems to resonate with the humorless and self-righteous combativeness that was the hallmark of his subject's political makeup and his stormy dealings with Congress. There was no disputing his "courage . . . and strength of purpose," English novelist Charles Dickens wrote of Johnson when he met him on a visit to America. At the same time, the writer noted, he seemed utterly devoid of any "genial sunlight."

This cartoon of Andrew Johnson was typical of many that appeared after Thaddeus Stevens, the Radical Republican leader, declared, "The President will be crowned King before the next Congress meets." The remark was occasioned by Johnson's conciliatory Reconstruction policy which had begun while Congress, who bitterly opposed him, was in recess.

The term "impeachment" does not mean removal from office. It is actually a parliamentary term for indictment. According to the Constitution, the House of Representatives has the sole power to impeach a president. The Senate is responsible for the trial. The removal of a president requires a two-thirds majority vote of senators in favor of conviction. On February 24, 1868, Andrew Johnson was the first and only president impeached by the House of Representatives in a vote of 126 to 47. According to Gideon Welles, the secretary of the navy, the charges were, "a mountain of words . . . but not even a mouse of impeachment material. . . . Those who may vote to convict . . . would as readily vote to impeach the President had he been accused of stepping on a dog's tail." The Senate acquitted Johnson by one vote. This is a photograph of the Managers of the House of Representatives who prosecuted Johnson's impeachment in the Senate trial.

When Andrew Johnson entered the United States Senate in 1856, he had reached the summit of his political ambition. But, although the Senate seat was enough to satisfy the aspirations of this self-educated tailor from Tennessee, he had yet higher peaks to climb. When the Civil War came in 1861, Johnson's dislike of slavery made him the only member of Congress from a seceding southern state to oppose withdrawal from the Union. Within his own state this made him a traitor. In the North, however, he became a hero. In 1862, Lincoln appointed him military governor of Tennessee, charged with restoring the state's civil authority. Johnson performed this job well, and his political fortunes took an upward leap.

A major concern among Republicans as they looked toward Lincoln's reelection in 1864 was that voters perceived Lincoln as too hostile to the South and therefore incapable of effecting the national reconciliation that was necessary as the Civil War drew to its close. In the face of that concern, it seemed that Johnson might be helpful in assuring Lincoln's reelection. In the hope that this man, who had just restored Tennessee to the Union, would allay voters' doubts about their presidential nominee, the Republicans named Johnson as Lincoln's running mate.

Had events run a normal course, this perhaps would have been the last that was heard of Johnson. After Lincoln's reelection, his new vice-president, having served his purpose in the campaign, would in all probability have sunk into quiet anonymity. But with the assassination of Lincoln in 1865, Johnson suddenly found himself in the White House.

Johnson's main task when he took office was the reconstruction of the defeated South. In shouldering this responsibility he favored the same conciliatory policy that Lincoln had, which in essence meant readmitting the South to the Union quickly while imposing on it only minimal retribution for making war on the Union. Congress's Radical Republican leadership, however, was not so charitable. While Johnson sought the South's reinstatement on easy terms, the Radicals called for the disenfranchising of many white southerners, aggressive protections for the rights of the region's newly freed blacks, and establishment of military governments throughout the South.

Unfortunately, Johnson was unable to reconcile his disagreements with Congress. As one historian put it, "his mind had one compartment for right and one for wrong, but no middle chamber where the two could commingle." When the Radicals began replacing his Reconstruction policies with harsher measures of their own, Johnson could, therefore, think of no alternative but to veto them. But, in the end, Congress not only overrode Johnson's vetoes, it also acquired a hearty dislike for him. In 1868, the House of Representatives voted to impeach him. At the subsequent Senate trial, however, the impeachment charges proved flimsy at best, and the Senate exonerated Johnson by a margin of one vote.

The victory was a hollow one. During the remainder of his term, Johnson's power to influence national policy was almost nonexistent. Nevertheless, he remained a self-righteous fighter to the end, and in his final message to Congress he roundly rebuked its members for their tyrannical treatment of the South.

BORN
Raleigh, North Carolina, December 29, 1808

ANCESTRY
Scottish-Irish and English

WIFE
Eliza McCardle
Born: Leesburg, Tennessee
October 4, 1810
Died: Greene County, Tennessee
January 15, 1876

MARRIED
Greeneville, Tennessee, December 17, 1827

CHILDREN
Martha (1828-1901?)
Charles (1830-1863)
Mary (1832-1883)
Robert (1834-1869)
Andrew (1852-1879)

HOME
Greeneville, Tennessee

EDUCATION
Self-educated

RELIGION
No denomination

OCCUPATIONS
Tailor and legislator

PREPRESIDENTIAL OFFICES
Alderman of Greeneville, Tennessee (1828-1830)
Mayor of Greeneville, Tennessee (1830-1834)
Member of the Tennessee Legislature
(1835-1837 and 1839-1843)
Member of the U.S. House of Representatives (1843-1853)
Governor of Tennessee (1853-1857)
Member of the U.S. Senate (1857-1862)
Military Governor of Tennessee (1862-1864)
Vice-President (1865)

POLITICAL PARTY
Democratic
Elected Vice-President, National Union ticket

INAUGURATED AS PRESIDENT
April 15, 1865, Kirkwood House, Washington, D.C.

AGE AT INAUGURATION
56

POSTPRESIDENTIAL OFFICES
Member of the U.S. Senate (1875)

DIED
Carter County, Tennessee, July 31, 1875, age 66

ULYSSES S. GRANT

When Thomas LeClear painted Ulysses S. Grant around 1880, he invested his subject with an authoritative elegance that contrasted sharply with the rumpled and unprepossessing quality of so many other Grant images. To some extent this may simply be the reflection of a greater dignity that came to Grant as he grew older. But whatever the reason, LeClear's likeness is a far cry from the way Grant was generally perceived during the Civil War.

This photograph of Ulysses S. Grant and his family was taken in 1883, a year before he lost his fortune in unwise investments. Two years later, stricken with cancer and wanting to provide his family with a source of income after his death, he struggled to complete his 295,000-word Personal Memoirs. Shortly before Grant finished, on July 16, 1885, he wrote to his doctor, "I am ready now to go at any time. I know there is nothing but suffering for me while I do live." One week later he was dead. The book would earn $450,000 within two years.

In contrast to so many other Union generals, Ulysses S. Grant got results; he won battles. Abraham Lincoln said of him, "I can't spare this man. He fights." When rumors of Grant's drinking reached Lincoln, he said that if he knew what brand of whisky Grant drank, he would send some to his other generals. Grant was appointed general of all the Union Armies in 1864 and presided over Confederate General Robert E. Lee's surrender at Appomattox. This 1865 painting, titled Grant and His Generals, was the work of Ole Peter Hansen Balling who based much of it on life portraits he had drawn of the generals at the front.

Much of the life of Ulysses Grant reads like a classic story of the square peg being forced to fit into a round hole. Accepted at West Point in 1839, he entered the Academy only because his father had pressured him. At his graduation four years later, his reputation for slovenly dress and reluctance to accept leadership responsibilities when they were offered to him seemed to mark him as a soldier destined for mediocre distinction at best. As a junior army officer, Grant only reinforced that prognosis. After serving creditably in the Mexican War, he gradually became bored with military life, and by the early 1850s the combination of prolonged absences from his wife and the tediousness of his duties at outposts in the far West had led to a drinking problem. Just how substantial this problem was and whether it was, as some claim, the factor that finally drove him from the army are debatable questions. But one thing is certain: By the time he resigned his captain's commission in 1854, he was more than ready to give up his career as a soldier.

Grant, however, fared less well out of uniform than he had in. A failure at farming, he later turned to selling real estate and bill collecting. When those ventures also ended poorly, he was reduced to helping his two younger brothers as a clerk in their leather shop in Galena, Illinois.

With the onset of the Civil War in 1861, Grant's sagging fortunes took a sharp turn for the better. Answering the Union's call to arms immediately, he achieved a general's rank within only a few months and was soon providing the North with some of its most crucial victories. Grant, the reluctant West Point cadet, had blossomed into a military genius. By early 1864, Lincoln entrusted him with command of all the Union armies, and by war's end his reputation as a chief architect of the North's triumph over the South made him one of the most revered men in America.

But just as it seemed that Grant had found his proper niche in life, the square-peg syndrome returned. Like Zachary Taylor following the Mexican War, Grant was now eminently ripe for a presidential nomination. In 1868, knowing they had a sure winner on their hands, the Republicans named him their White House candidate by acclamation and, as expected, Grant emerged from the final election a hands-down winner.

Unfortunately, when Grant assumed the presidency, the dogged aggressiveness that had characterized him in Civil War combat deserted him and was replaced by a trusting tractability. He was all too willing to place the fate of his administration in the hands of others, who all too often were rapaciously self-serving cronies and businessmen. Thus, Grant's presidency quickly became a hotbed of corruption, and as his appointees—ranging from a secretary of war to local postal officials—enriched themselves with bribes and rake-offs, "Grantism" became synonymous with violation of the public trust.

Yet Grant's personal reputation suffered barely a scratch from the disclosures of this malfeasance. A scrupulously honest man himself, he had no trouble winning reelection in 1872. Moreover, in 1880, support for a third nomination was strong enough to make him frontrunner, and had he run, it is not altogether impossible that the electorate would have given him a third term.

BORN
Point Pleasant, Ohio, April 27, 1822

ANCESTRY
English-Scottish

WIFE
Julia Boggs Dent
Born: St. Louis, Missouri
January 26, 1826
Died: Washington, D.C.
December 14, 1902

MARRIED
St. Louis, Missouri, August 22, 1848

CHILDREN
Frederick Dent (1850-1912)
Ulysses Simpson (1852-1929)
Ellen Wrenshall (1855-1922)
Jesse Root (1858-1934)

EDUCATION
U.S. Military Academy, West Point, New York (1843)

RELIGION
Methodist

OCCUPATIONS
Soldier, farmer, real-estate agent, custom house clerk, and store clerk

MILITARY SERVICE
Commissioned Second Lieutenant, 4th U.S. Infantry (1843)
Resigned as captain (1854)
Reentered army in August 1861, rose from brigadier general to general in chief of Union armies on March 12, 1864, resigned 1869

POLITICAL PARTY
Republican

INAUGURATED AS PRESIDENT
First term: March 4, 1869, the Capitol, Washington, D.C.
Second term: March 4, 1873, the Capitol, Washington, D.C.

AGE AT INAUGURATION
46

DIED
Mount McGregor, New York, July 23 1885, age 63

RUTHERFORD B. HAYES

NINETEENTH PRESIDENT   1877–1881

Olin Warner sculpted this bust of Rutherford B. Hayes in the late summer of 1876 with the intention of convincing the Republican party to use replicas of it to promote Hayes's presidential candidacy. At least one party official thought this was a scheme worth considering, and, in support of it, he noted to a fellow campaign worker: "The idea is prevalent even in Republican ranks that [Hayes] is a second-rate man. The bust convinces the beholder that he is a man of power." Since only a few versions of Warner's likeness are known to exist today, it would seem that the replicating venture never went much beyond the talking stage.

Samuel J. Tilden, who was defeated by Hayes in the disputed presidential election of 1876, was a brilliant lawyer who rose to prominence in the Democratic party as a champion of government reform. From 1866 to 1874, he was chairman of the New York State Democratic committee and succeeded in ridding New York City of corrupt politicians and cleaning up the state's judicial and governmental bodies. In 1874 he became governor and while in office did much to improve the state's corrupted fiscal system. When Tilden died, in 1886, he bequeathed his fortune to create the New York Public Library.

Lucy Hayes, the first First Lady to hold a college degree, was the mother of seven sons and one daughter. It was she who began the tradition of the annual Easter-egg rolling on the lawn of the White House. Mrs. Hayes also supported temperance and banned alcoholic beverages at 1600 Pennsylvania Avenue. The result was many dull evenings in Washington and her nickname—Lemonade Lucy. This photograph was taken in 1878 when she was forty-seven years old.

On election night of 1876, when the Democrats' presidential candidate, New York governor Samuel J. Tilden, went to bed he thought that he had just won the nation's highest office. Soon after the polls were closed and the ballots were counted, however, Republicans charged that Tilden's majority vote in several states was the result of fraud at the polls and that their candidate, Ohio governor Rutherford B. Hayes, had really won the contest. Charge followed countercharge, and eventually arbitration of the dispute was submitted to a special congressional commission, which, after much behind-the-scenes wheeling and dealing, declared Hayes the winner.

Resigned to accepting the commission's decision, Democrats were understandably unhappy with the outcome and, in many quarters, Hayes became know as "His Fraudulency." But although the legitimacy of his presidency remained a question throughout Hayes's administration, this congenial but decidedly uncharismatic man proved to be an extremely able chief executive. Considering that he faced Democratic majorities in both House and Senate through much of his term in office, the list of his accomplishments is all the more impressive.

It was Hayes who, for example, ended the Reconstruction policies that Congress had imposed on the South after the Civil War. The federal troops stationed in that region were withdrawn, thus terminating "carpetbag" state governments often ruled by unscrupulous northern politicians and setting in motion the final reconciliation of North and South. Hayes also took the first significant step to curb the "spoils system," which had largely reduced the civil service to a body of political hacks whose only virtue was their loyalty to the party in power. To Hayes's credit as well was his choice of unusually talented men as his advisers. Among his wisest selections was Secretary of Treasury John Sherman, with whom Hayes adroitly managed to stave off the potential fiscal damage of a congressional act calling for an inflationary currency policy. Finally, through the use of his veto power, he succeeded in thwarting efforts of congressional Democrats to minimize the influence of the Republican-leaning black vote in the South by curtailing federal oversight of national elections in the region.

For all its constructiveness, however, Hayes's brand of leadership did not make him especially well regarded by the politicians within his own party. While some fellow Republicans berated him for restoring the South to self-rule, others bitterly resented his drive to transform the civil service into a meritocracy. And, when it became clear that Hayes would not seek a second term, the response from many Republicans was "good riddance!"

Had the anti-Hayes Republicans looked beyond their short-term interests and biases, however, they might have seen that in one important respect Hayes served his party well. It was his impeccably honest administration that gave a new polish to the Republican image so badly tarnished by the scandals of the previous presidency.

R.B.Hayes

BORN
Delaware, Ohio, October 4, 1822

ANCESTRY
English-Scottish

WIFE
Lucy Ware Webb
Born: Chillicothe, Ohio
August 28, 1831
Died: Fremont, Ohio
June 25, 1889

MARRIED
Cincinnati, Ohio, December 30, 1852

CHILDREN
Birchard Austin (1853-1926)
Webb Cook (1856-1934)
Rutherford Platt (1858-1927)
Joseph Thompson (1861-1863)
George Crook (1864-1866)
Fanny (1866-1950)
Scott Russell (1871-1923)
Manning Force (1873-1874)

HOME
Spiegel Grove, Fremont, Ohio

EDUCATION
Kenyon College, Gambier, Ohio; B.A. (1842)
Harvard Law School, Cambridge, Massachusetts; LL.B. (1845)

RELIGION
Methodist

OCCUPATIONS
Lawyer, politician, philanthropist, and president of National Prison Association

MILITARY SERVICE
Rose from major to major general, 23rd Ohio volunteers (1861-1865)

PREPRESIDENTIAL OFFICES
City Solicitor of Cincinnati (1858-1861)
Member of the the House of Representatives (1865-1867)
Governor of Ohio (1868-1872 and 1876-1877)

POLITICAL PARTY
Republican

INAUGURATED AS PRESIDENT
March 3, 1877, the White House in a private ceremony
March 5, 1877, the Capitol, Washington, D.C.

AGE AT INAUGURATION
54

DIED
Fremont, Ohio, January 17, 1893, age 70

JAMES A. GARFIELD

TWENTIETH PRESIDENT   1881

Ole Peter Hansen Balling's sedately restrained portrait of James A. Garfield does not capture the full magnitude of the power that this man could sometimes exercise over his contemporaries. Perhaps no likeness could, for Garfield was at his most impressive when speaking before an audience. As he moved toward the climax of a speech, artfully mixing logic with flights of metaphor, an admirer once noted, his thoughts often seemed to pour forth "like solid shot from a cannon."

President Garfield was shot by Charles S. Guiteau on July 2, 1881, four months after his inauguration, and died on September 19, 1881. The bullet had lodged in a back muscle and did not require removal. The doctors, unaware of this, probed futilely for it, using unsanitary instruments and spreading infection which weakened and finally killed him. This mourning ribbon commemorates his untimely death.

Before his election to the presidency, a Milwaukee newspaper stated that James Garfield "is exceptionally clean for a man who has been engaged for twenty years in active politics." Garfield was a deeply religious man who built his political career upon his fame as an evangelical preacher. He is shown right in 1881 with his family, including his mother, his wife, and five of their seven children.

In the late 1850s, the young James Garfield was a respected lay preacher and teacher-principal at northern Ohio's Western Reserve Eclectic Institute. It seemed, therefore, that if he was to make a significant mark in life, it would be in education or religion. But beneath the outward signs that he had found his proper vocational niche, Garfield was restless. In 1859, armed with an unusual flair for the grandiloquent turn of phrase, he decided to enter politics. Four years later, after serving in the Ohio legislature and as a colonel in the Union army, he won a seat in the House of Representatives.

Garfield rose rapidly in the House hierarchy and eventually became an influential member of the Radical Republican circles that opposed Andrew Johnson's lenient treatment of the war-torn South after the Civil War. By the late 1870s, he was serving as his party's minority leader in the House.

Unlike so many others who attain influence in American politics, Garfield harbored no presidential ambitions. Instead, the only office to which he aspired was a seat in the Senate. Just as he was about to gain that position, however, there was an unexpected turn of events. In 1880, with the Republicans split into two factions—the "Stalwarts" led by Roscoe Conkling and the "Half-Breeds" led by James G. Blaine—the party became hopelessly deadlocked at its national convention over the nomination of a presidential candidate. Unable to choose between the Half-Breeds' Blaine and Stalwart favorite Ulysses Grant, the delegates finally decided, after thirty-five ballots, that a compromise was in order. Two ballots later, Garfield emerged as the Republican standard-bearer and, as a sop to the Stalwarts, the party shortly thereafter chose Conkling's protégé Chester A. Arthur to be his vice-presidential running mate.

Garfield's nomination did not end his party's squabblings, which had little to do with ideology and a great deal to do with power and, above all, with political patronage. Thus, when Garfield won the election, the foremost question in the minds of Stalwarts and Half-Breeds was who would win the greatest favor from the new patronage-dispensing president.

The answer to that question proved especially disappointing to Stalwart Roscoe Conkling. Not only did Garfield name his rival James G. Blaine secretary of state; he also dared to appoint non-Stalwarts to the New York City Customs House where, as senator from New York, Conkling felt he had every right to dictate the choices. The Garfield-Conkling clash over this matter might be merely an amusing anecdote if it had simply ended when Conkling resigned his Senate seat and then failed in his plan to rebuke Garfield by being promptly reelected. Unfortunately, it did not. On July 2, 1881, as the president was about to board a train in Washington, Charles Guiteau, a mentally unstable Conkling follower, drew a pistol and, shouting, "I am a Stalwart and now Chester Arthur is President!" shot Garfield in the back. Eleven weeks later, Garfield died from his wounds.

Something positive did, however, result from this tragedy. In its wake came the realization that if quarrels over federal patronage could lead to a presidential assassination, then something had to be done to stop them. Two years after Garfield's death, Congress passed the Civil Service Reform Act, which represented the first significant step in eliminating the spoils system from the country's civil service.

BORN
Orange Township, Cuyahoga County, Ohio,
November 19, 1831

ANCESTRY
English and French Huguenot

WIFE
Lucretia Rudolph
Born: Hiram, Ohio
April 19, 1832
Died: Pasadena, California
March 14, 1918

MARRIED
Hiram, Ohio, November 11, 1858

CHILDREN
Eliza Arabella (1860-1863)
Harry Augustus (1863-1942)
James Rudolph (1865-1950)
Mary (1867-1947)
Irvin McDowell (1870-1951)
Abram (1872-1958)
Edward (1874-1876)

HOME
Lawnfield, Mentor, Ohio

EDUCATION
Williams College, Williamstown, Massachussets; B.A. (1856)

RELIGION
Disciples of Christ

OCCUPATIONS
Sailor, school teacher, soldier, and
president of Hiram College

MILITARY SERVICE
Rose from lieutenant colonel to major general,
42nd Ohio Volunteers (1861-1863)

PREPRESIDENTIAL OFFICES
Member of the Ohio Senate (1859-1861)
Member of the U.S. House of Representatives (1863-1880)
Chairman of the House Committee on Appropriations
(1871-1880)
Minority Leader in U.S. House of Representatives
(1877-1880)

POLITICAL PARTY
Republican

INAUGURATED AS PRESIDENT
March 4, 1881, the Capitol, Washington, D.C.

AGE AT INAUGURATION
49

DIED
Elberon, N.J., September 19, 1881, age 49

CHESTER A. ARTHUR

TWENTY-FIRST PRESIDENT   1881–1885

Chester A. Arthur may well have been the most elegantly turned out president ever to sit in the White House. With his muttonchop whiskers "invariably trimmed to the perfection point" and his scrupulously tailored suits made of only the finest fabrics, he personified the ideal Victorian gentleman.

When President Garfield was assassinated in 1881, there was great doubt about his successor's leadership qualities. But four years later Mark Twain said, "I am but one of fifty-five million; still, in the opinion of this one-fifty-five millionth of the country's population, it would be hard indeed to better President Arthur's Administration." The bandanna left is from the 1880 presidential election.

The New York Republican hierarchy through which Chester Arthur rose rested on two basic foundation stones. One was the system of patronage politics of which he proved a master during his tenure as the job-dispensing customs collector of the Port of New York. The other was the mutually rewarding relationship that Arthur's party cultivated with the great industrial and banking entrepreneurs of the day. The "Kings of Wall Street," pictured here, were not just the titans of finance who led the nation's great economic expansion after the Civil War. Many of them, including Jay Gould and William Vanderbilt, seated opposite each other at the table, were also primary players in the game of granting financial favor to public officials in exchange for preferential treatment of their interests in courts and legislatures.

"I have but one annoyance with the administration of President Arthur," New York's Republican boss Roscoe Conkling declared in 1883, "and that is that, in contrast with it, the Administration of Hayes becomes respectable, if not heroic." Coming from Conkling, who was always rabidly anti-Hayes, this was, indeed, harsh condemnation of Chester Arthur's presidential performance. Yet it did not truly reflect the deep bitterness that Conkling felt toward Arthur then. For in supporting the Pendleton Act of 1883, which called for the elimination of the spoils system from much of the civil service, Arthur had taken a landmark step toward undercutting the power that Conkling enjoyed because of his control over so many choice government appointments.

The most outrageous aspect of this, from Conkling's point of view, was that Chester Arthur was himself a product of the very patronage machine he was helping to destroy. Even more galling, it was to Conkling that Arthur owed his rise through that system. When, for example, the chief customs position for New York City fell vacant in 1871, Conkling maneuvered Arthur into that job, which brought with it a handsome income and control over more than one thousand other customs appointments. Then, in 1877, when the Hayes administration had sought Arthur's removal from this post, Conkling again came to Arthur's aid and led the fight—albeit unsuccessfully—to block his friend's dismissal. Finally, although Conkling had urged Arthur to refuse the Republican nomination of 1880 as James Garfield's vice-presidential running mate, there could be no denying that the delegates accorded this honor to Arthur because of his close identification with Conkling. When Arthur succeeded to the White House, following Garfield's death in 1881, it was fair to say that in large degree he owed this unexpected elevation to his boss Conkling.

Although Chester Arthur was largely a creature of Conkling's making, he did not lack a will of his own. Nor did he share Conkling's broad tolerance for the political jobbery and chicanery that characterized the spoils system of the late nineteenth century. Thus, in addition to putting the weight of his presidency behind the Pendleton Act, Arthur pressed vigorously for a complete investigation of rampant fraud in the nation's western postal system. He also proved to be an enemy of congressional "pork barreling," and when a bill for river and harbor improvements reached his desk, he vetoed it, claiming that it was merely a vehicle for securing special-interest votes for incumbent congressmen in their home states.

As a result of these efforts to put government on a more honest footing, Arthur's presidency proved to be a great surprise to all factions. For the Republican party's spoils-minded bosses, the astonishment took the form of embittered shock that one of their own should dare to betray their interests. The surprise was decidedly more pleasant in nature, however, for those concerned with cleaning up the corruption that had plagued the federal government since the scandal-ridden Grant administration. Although Chester Arthur did not entirely eradicate that corruption, he curbed it substantially and certainly far more than his spoilsman's origin had suggested he would.

BORN
North Fairfield, Vermont, October 5, 1830

ANCESTRY
Scottish-Irish and English

WIFE
Ellen Lewis Herndon
Born: Fredericksburg, Virginia
August 30, 1837
Died: New York City, New York
January 12, 1880

MARRIED
New York City, New York, October 25, 1859

CHILDREN
William Lewis Herndon (1860-1863)
Chester Alan Jr. (1864-1937)
Ellen (1871-1915)

HOME
New York City, New York

EDUCATION
Union College, Schenectady, New York; B.A. (1848),
M.A. (1851)

RELIGION
Episcopalian

OCCUPATIONS
Teacher, school principal, and lawyer

MILITARY SERVICE
Quartermaster general and inspector general for Union
forces (1861-1862)

PREPRESIDENTIAL OFFICES
New York Collector of Customs (1871-1878)
Vice-President (1881)

POLITICAL PARTY
Republican

INAUGURATED AS PRESIDENT
September 20, 1881, New York City, New York

AGE AT INAUGURATION
50

DIED
New York City, New York, November 18, 1886, age 56

GROVER CLEVELAND

TWENTY-SECOND PRESIDENT 1885–1889
TWENTY-FOURTH PRESIDENT 1893–1897

In 1899, when Anders Zorn completed his paired likenesses of Grover and Frances Cleveland, the former president felt that the painter had not done full justice to his beautiful wife. On the other hand, having never harbored a shred of vanity in the matter of his own appearance, he was quite content with Zorn's unaggrandizing treatment of him. "As for my ugly mug," he told a friend, "I think the artist has 'struck it off' in great shape."

The bandanna above is from Grover Cleveland's presidential campaign of 1884 in which he defeated Republican James G. Blaine. He was the only Democratic president from 1869 to 1913 and the only president in the history of the United States to serve two nonconsecutive terms.

When twenty-one-year-old Frances Folsom married forty-nine-year-old Grover Cleveland on June 2, 1886, in a private ceremony at the White House, it generated great public interest. Frances, pictured above in her wedding dress, was the daughter of one of Cleveland's law partners; she became Cleveland's ward after her father died in 1875. The tall and beautiful First Lady charmed Washington society and the press with her unaffected and lively personality. There was a noticeable change in the President, too. Before he married, he was known as an irascible but honest politician who worked hard but was disinclined to take bold initiatives. Afterward he became more sociable, was less irritable, and, most important, displayed a more positive and aggressive style of leadership as evidenced in his later battles with Congress over the issue of tariffs.

When New York governor Grover Cleveland first heard of the mounting enthusiasm among Democrats for his presidential nomination in 1884, he was chagrined. But in a climate of freewheeling enterprise, when elected officials routinely sold themselves to the nearest influence-seeking industrial plutocrat, Cleveland had an asset that made him an eminently desirable White House candidate: He was a man of unflinching honesty. The Democrats saw in that rectitude their first real chance in the twenty-three years since the Civil War to capture the presidency.

After Cleveland was nominated, however, the Democrats found that their candidate's closet was not skeleton-free. When the story emerged that he had fathered a child out of wedlock in his youth, the Republican opposition made the most of it. But Republican presidential hopeful James G. Blaine also had a skeleton in his closet. There were allegations that during his years in Congress he had accepted a number of bribes from the railroads. As a result, in 1884 the voters found they had to choose between a man accused of private indiscretion and a man charged with violating the public trust. By the slimmest of margins, they cast their lot with Grover Cleveland.

As his presidency unfolded, it soon became clear that Cleveland would fully measure up to his reputation as the honest protector of the public interest. Under pressure from him, federal lands, which the railroads had wrongfully claimed as subsidies for the building of their lines, were opened to homesteading. At the same time, his administration undertook to hasten the civil service reforms that had begun during the Hayes and Arthur presidencies. Moreover, Cleveland proved painfully conscientious in finding sound men to sit on the new Interstate Commerce Commission to monitor railroad rates in the public interest. Unfortunately, the positive feelings that these actions engendered suddenly weakened when, toward the end of his first term, Cleveland pressed Congress for reductions in the nation's high protective tariffs. In the wake of cries that Cleveland's tariff proposal would destroy the country's industrial prosperity, he failed to win his reelection bid in 1888.

Cleveland's presidential career was, however, by no means over. Four years later, the electorate returned him to the White House. But Cleveland might have been better off remaining in retirement. By early 1893, the country was entering a deep economic depression, and whatever he did to meet various phases of that crisis seemed only to alienate his supporters. Thus, by ordering troops to Chicago to maintain order during the Pullman strike of 1894 and by allowing his attorney general to bring legal action against the strike's leaders, he lost whatever support he had among organized labor. Even more damaging to Cleveland were his monetary policies, and after opposing inflationary measures for raising the incomes of sorely pressed farmers and workers, he found himself denounced as a pawn of the moneyed elite. By far, the loudest protest against Cleveland's anti-inflationary stand came from populist elements in his own party. Consequently, as these inflationists gained dominance among Democrats during the final year of his presidency, Cleveland suffered the ultimate humiliation of being an outcast within the party he had once led.

BORN
Caldwell, New Jersey, March 18, 1837

ANCESTRY
Irish-English-French

WIFE
Frances Folsom
Born: Buffalo, New York
July 21, 1864
Died: Baltimore, Maryland
October 29, 1947

MARRIED
White House, Washington, D.C., June 2, 1886

CHILDREN
Ruth (1891-1904)
Esther (1893-1980)
Marion (1895-1977)
Richard Folsom (1897-1974)
Francis Grover (1903-   )

EDUCATION
Public Schools

RELIGION
Presbyterian

OCCUPATIONS
Lawyer and Princeton University trustee

PREPRESIDENTIAL OFFICES
Erie County Assistant District Attorney (1863-1865)
Sheriff of Erie County (1871-1873)
Mayor of Buffalo (1882)
Governor of New York (1883-1885)

POLITICAL PARTY
Democratic

INAUGURATED AS PRESIDENT
First term: March 4, 1885, the Capitol, Washington, D.C.
Second term: March 4, 1893, the Capitol, Washington, D.C.

AGE AT INAUGURATION
47

DIED
Princeton, New Jersey, June 24, 1908, age 71

BENJAMIN HARRISON

TWENTY-THIRD PRESIDENT 1889–1893

This drawing of Benjamin Harrison is believed to be Eastman Johnson's preliminary sketch for the substantial oil portrait that today hangs in the White House. In 1895, when Harrison arrived in New York from Indianapolis to pose for Johnson, he had been out of the White House for two years and was quite content with life away from the public eye. Nevertheless, newspapers interpreted Harrison's visit to Johnson as a pretext for cultivating interest in his renomination among eastern Republicans.

Shortly after Queen Liliuokalani claimed the throne in Hawaii in 1891 and renounced her island nation's pro-American constitution, Sanford Dole, an American planter, joined the United States Minister to Hawaii in a conspiracy to make the country an American protectorate. An enthusiastic expansionist, President Harrison endorsed the resulting treaty of annexation. The Senate, however, failed to vote its approval, and President Cleveland later withdrew the agreement from consideration. The photograph of Queen Liliuokalani above was taken in 1908.

Benjamin Harrison capitalized on the memory of his grandfather, William Henry Harrison, the ninth president of the United States, to help him win the presidential election of 1888. He successfully utilized the log cabin motif associated with his grandfather in campaign devices like the ball right, which was rolled around the countryside.

When the Whig party nominated William Henry Harrison for president in 1840, there was little in his background to qualify him, except for his record as an Indian fighter and general in the War of 1812. In 1888, when the Republicans settled on his grandson, Benjamin, it seemed that history was repeating itself.

Although not quite the political nonentity that his grandfather had been, Benjamin Harrison was hardly a man of longtime prominence in national politics. Aside from serving one unremarkable term in the Senate and once running unsuccessfully for the Indiana governorship, his only distinction was that he was a safe, clean, and loyal Republican. But apparently that, combined with being the grandson of "Old Tippecanoe" and the citizen of a swing state, provided Harrison with enough cachet to make the Republicans think they could sell him to the electorate. And, indeed, they were right; on March 4, 1889, having convinced the public that the key to American prosperity was his party's promise to maintain a high protective tariff, Harrison took the presidential oath of office.

About two weeks later, a Washington journalist wrote of him, "he is narrow, unresponsive, and oh, so cold. . . . As one Senator says: 'It's like talking to a hitching post.'"

This may have been overly harsh, but it was soon clear that a hallmark of Harrison's presidential style was an aloof and sometimes icy detachment from the political fray. This did not mean that he was a presidential idler. To the contrary, he proved to be an unusually hard-working chief executive, known for his attentiveness to detail. What it did mean, however, was that Harrison played an essentially passive role in many of the events of his administration. While, for example, he supported such measures as the McKinley Tariff and the first federal attempt to curb industrial monopoly, the Sherman Antitrust Act, he had very little to do with their actual making. Moreover, despite his abhorrence of efforts in the South to bar blacks from voting in federal elections, he refused to take an aggressive stand to prevent this disenfranchisement. Finally, like many other mainstream politicians of the day, Harrison proved all too willing to ignore the protests of workers and farmers who claimed that they were being denied a share in the nation's prosperity.

Although Harrison did not distinguish himself as a molder of domestic policy, he did play an active role in moving the country toward greater involvement with the rest of the world. It could be said that Harrison's support for a modernized navy and the strong posturing of his administration in various international disputes were harbingers of the emergence of the United States as a world power after 1900.

Harrison, who never particularly relished being president, consented to run for a second term in 1892 only out of a sense of obligation to his party. But growing voter restiveness over the Republicans' tendency to cater to the interests of big business prevented his reelection. As a staunchly loyal member of his party, Harrison was somewhat disturbed at this outcome, but from a purely personal point of view, the defeat, as he told a friend, carried "no sting."

BORN
North Bend, Ohio, August 20, 1833

ANCESTRY
English-Scottish

GRANDFATHER
William Henry Harrison, ninth president

FIRST WIFE
Caroline (Carrie) Lavinia Scott
Born: Oxford, Ohio
October 1, 1832
Died: Washington, D.C.
October 25, 1892

SECOND WIFE
Mary Scott Lord Dimmick
Born: Honestdale, Pennsylvania
April 30, 1858
Died: New York City, New York
January 5, 1948

MARRIED
First marriage: Oxford, Ohio, October 20, 1853
Second marriage: New York City, New York, April 6, 1896

CHILDREN
By first wife:
Russell Benjamin (1854-1936)
Mary Scott (1858-1930)
By second wife:
Elizabeth (1897-1955)

EDUCATION
Miami University, Oxford, Ohio; B.A. (1852)
Studied law with Benjamin Storer, Cincinnati, Ohio
(1852-1854)

RELIGION
Presbyterian

OCCUPATIONS
Lawyer, notary public, and soldier

MILITARY SERVICE
Rose from second lieutenant to brigadier general,
70th Indiana Volunteers (1862-1865)

PREPRESIDENTIAL OFFICES
City Attorney (1857)
Secretary of the Indiana Republican Central Committee
(1858-1860)
State Supreme Court Reporter (1861-1862)
Member of the U.S. Senate (1881-1887)

POLITICAL PARTY
Republican

INAUGURATED AS PRESIDENT
March 4, 1889, the Capitol, Washington, D.C.

AGE AT INAUGURATION
55

DIED
Indianapolis, Indiana, March 13, 1901, age 67

WILLIAM McKINLEY

TWENTY-FIFTH PRESIDENT   1897–1901

A historian once remarked that the pale-complected William McKinley had the demeanor of a "benign undertaker." Judging from his portrait by August Benziger, that description, in some respects at least, does seem apt. But funereal exterior notwithstanding, McKinley was an unusually warm and charming individual. Henry Adams called him a "marvelous manager of men," and another Washington observer claimed that "he met angrily insistent men . . . at his office door" and invariably "sent them away beaming."

Although William McKinley said he had had enough of the presidency after one term, he ran for reelection in 1900. The Democrats again nominated William Jennings Bryan, whose continuing advocacy of a silver-backed currency had become irrelevant in light of the nation's prosperity. Theodore Roosevelt, a hero of the Spanish-American War and the popular governor of New York, was added to the Republican ticket to assure McKinley's reelection. Shown above is an umbrella from that presidential campaign.

William McKinley's administration inaugurated the age of American imperialism. The United States had become a player in world affairs with the Spanish-American War which resulted in the American control of Guam, the Philippines, and Puerto Rico. (Hawaii, Wake Island, and several of the islands of Samoa were acquired later.) The Open Door policy in 1899 marked the beginning of American influence in China. This photograph shows McKinley with his Cabinet, including Secretary of State John M. Hay, center, and Secretary of War Elihu Root, to Hay's right, the architects of American imperialism.

As the severe depression spawned by the Panic of 1893 continued into 1896, it seemed to many people that the presidential election that year represented an Armageddon involving two distinctly different ways of dealing with the nation's economic woes. For William Jennings Bryan, the Democrats' White House hopeful, the key to increasing the deplorably depressed incomes of workers and farmers was an inflationary scheme to replace the country's gold monetary standard with the coinage of silver at a ratio of sixteen to one with gold. For William McKinley, the Republican presidential nominee, however, such a measure threatened disaster. So, while Bryan rallied voters with his warning that "you shall not crucify mankind upon a cross of gold," McKinleyites predicted that the day "sixteen to one" became law was the day grass would sprout in the streets of every American city.

The 1896 fight over silver and gold was one of the most impassioned battles in the history of presidential elections. But in the end, McKinley's solid reputation as an influential Ohio congressman engendered considerably more confidence than Bryan's evangelical defense of silver. Although McKinley did not claim the White House in a landslide, he certainly won it by a safe margin.

Despite the campaign's all-consuming debate about the way to restore American prosperity, McKinley's administration never had to grapple very hard with that issue. Gradually, the hard times of the mid-nineties began to recede more or less of their own accord. Instead, the main challenge facing McKinley lay in that jingoistic and vocal segment of the public which was urging active American support for the Cuban revolt against Spanish colonial rule.

Initially, McKinley adamantly opposed such interference. But when the United States battleship *Maine* blew up early in 1898 in Cuba's Havana harbor and when the press blamed the tragedy on the Spanish, popular sympathy for the Cuban rebels rapidly turned into a call for war with Spain that McKinley found impossible to deny. Within a few months, American forces had defeated the Spanish in both Cuba and the Philippine Islands.

This was not the end of it, however. As victor in the Spanish-American War, the United States was suddenly heir to some of the last vestiges of Spain's colonial empire, the Philippines and Puerto Rico. Despite the advice of members of his administration, who considered the Philippines a great asset in promoting American trading interests in the Pacific, McKinley was reluctant to accept these territorial spoils. But, at the same time, he was an unusually attentive reader of public opinion. Consequently, upon finding popular sentiment running heavily in favor of an overseas empire, he finally acquiesced to American annexation of the two territories. In so doing, he ushered the United States into an era that marked its emergence as a world power.

Unfortunately, McKinley was not to play any role in the new era. In September 1901, just a day after he had delivered a speech declaring that America's traditionally isolationist foreign policies were no longer possible, he was shot by an anarchist while attending a reception in Buffalo. Eight days later he was dead.

BORN
Niles, Ohio, January 29, 1843

ANCESTRY
English-Scottish-Irish-German

WIFE
Ida Saxton
Born: Canton, Ohio
June 8, 1847
Died: Canton, Ohio
May 26, 1907

MARRIED
Canton, Ohio, January 25, 1871

CHILDREN
Katherine (1871-1875)
Ida (1873-1873)

EDUCATION
Attended Allegheny College, Meadville, Pennsylvania
(1859-1860)
Attended Albany Law School, Albany, New York
(1866-1867)

RELIGION
Methodist

OCCUPATIONS
Teacher, soldier, and lawyer

MILITARY SERVICE
Rose to rank of major, 23rd Ohio Volunteers (1861-1865)

PREPRESIDENTIAL OFFICES
Prosecuting attorney of Stark County, Ohio (1869-1871)
Member of the U.S. House of Representatives
(1877-1883 and 1885-1891)
Governor of Ohio (1892-1896)

POLITICAL PARTY
Republican

INAUGURATED AS PRESIDENT
First term: March 4, 1897, the Capitol, Washington, D.C.
Second term: March 4, 1901, the Capitol, Washington, D.C.

AGE AT INAUGURATION
54

DIED
Buffalo, New York, September 14, 1901, age 58

THEODORE ROOSEVELT

TWENTY-SIXTH PRESIDENT   1901–1909

In his unrelenting vitality and his use of the presidency to create a more equitable balance between big business and the community at large, Theodore Roosevelt embodied for many of his contemporaries the essence of America's promise. Among those seeing him in that light were the organizers of New York City's Jacob Riis Settlement House. In 1905, they commissioned sculptor Sally Farnham to model this bronze relief likeness of Roosevelt for its gymnasium to serve as an inspiration to the newly arrived immigrants who used the facility.

Theodore Roosevelt, pictured here on his trip of 1906 to inspect the progress of the construction of the Panama Canal, was the first president to leave the country while in office. The Canal was an important part of Roosevelt's expansionist policy, and the events leading to its realization exemplified the aggressive use of American power which characterized his foreign policy. The United States had won the right to build the canal by actively promoting Panama's quest for independence from Colombia. Although Roosevelt's actions on this occasion were ethically questionable, the Canal was commercially and strategically essential to the United States as it developed into a world power.

The wild and colorful Roosevelt family, shown at left in this 1903 photograph, was extremely popular with the public. The five younger Roosevelts, who were called "the White House Gang," overran the presidential mansion with their playmates, including Jonathan Edwards, a bear, and Father Grady, a guinea pig. Roosevelt, once asked if he could control his lively and precocious eldest daughter, Alice, standing center (who had a penchant for cigarettes and snakes), replied, "I can be President of the United States or I can control Alice. I cannot possibly do both." Edith Roosevelt, the calm and elegant First Lady, managed to keep the household on an even keel.

Theodore Roosevelt was an amalgam of explosive energy and undauntable determination. In his youth, he suffered severely from asthma, but unwilling to accept this handicap, he embarked on a fitness program that would make him the most athletic president the United States has ever seen. By the time he graduated from Harvard, he was on his way to becoming a much-respected amateur naturalist and to producing a book on naval operations in the War of 1812 that is still a basic source for historians. When advised that public office seeking was an unfit pursuit for well-born gentlemen such as himself, he ran for office anyway and, as a member of the New York state legislature in the early 1880s, was soon making himself known as an outspoken foe of corruption in government.

A few years later, Roosevelt was roping steers on his ranch in the Dakota Badlands. By the early 1890s, he was a member of the United States Civil Service Commission, where his passionate opposition to patronage made him the bane of political spoilsmen. When the Spanish-American War broke out, he was serving as assistant secretary of the navy. But, not content with sitting out this conflict at a desk, he was soon raising his own regiment of Rough Riders and, on July 1, 1898, was leading a victorious charge up Cuba's San Juan Hill. Next seen, he was residing in New York's governor's mansion, where, thanks to his aggressive enthusiasm for various labor and business reforms, he found himself locked in constant combat with Thomas Platt, the conservative boss of his own Republican party.

In 1900, however, when Platt succeeded in ridding himself of the troublesome Roosevelt by engineering his nomination as William McKinley's vice-presidential running mate, it appeared that Teddy Roosevelt's political career had run out of steam, for with McKinley's election, Roosevelt seemed relegated to four years of anonymity. But when McKinley was assassinated in 1901, that prospect changed drastically and Roosevelt occupied an office in which his inexhaustible drive to achieve and dominate could enjoy free rein.

And achieve and dominate he did. In response to a mounting call for more protection of workers and the general public against the excesses of big business, Roosevelt applied his presidential influence with unprecedented vigor and a "big stick." Under his aegis, the largely dormant Sherman Antitrust Act became an effective means for curbing industrial monopolies, and Congress enacted laws putting new bite into the regulatory powers of the Interstate Commerce Commission. At the same time, Roosevelt's intervention in the massive coal strike of 1902 represented the first instance in which a chief executive took an active role in labor arbitration.

In foreign policy, Roosevelt proved equally forceful. When, for example, Colombia refused to endorse a treaty permitting the United States to build a canal through its Isthmus of Panama, he simply sought his canal-building agreement elsewhere. Soon his administration was helping Panama win its independence, and, with that achieved, a grateful Panama gave him his treaty.

But the most striking aspect of Roosevelt's administration was not what he did, but rather how he did it. For Roosevelt possessed an exuberance that inspired a turn-of-the-century optimism that the United States, with all its growing wealth and know-how, could achieve anything it wanted to.

BORN
New York City, New York, October 27, 1858
ANCESTRY
Dutch-Scottish-English-French Huguenot
FIRST WIFE
Alice Hathaway Lee
Born: Chestnut Hill, Massachusetts
July 29, 1861
Died: New York City, New York
February 14, 1884
SECOND WIFE
Edith Kermit Carow
Born: Norwich, Connecticut
August 6, 1861
Died: Oyster Bay, New York
September 30, 1948
MARRIED
First marriage: Brookline, Massachusetts, October 27, 1880
Second marriage: London, England, December 2, 1886
CHILDREN

By first wife:
Alice Lee (1884-1980)

By second wife:
Theodore (1887-1944)
Kermit (1889-1943)
Ethel Carow (1891-1977)
Archibald Bulloch (1894-1979)
Quentin (1897-1918)

HOME
28 East 20th Street, New York City, New York
Sagamore Hill, Oyster Bay, New York
EDUCATION
Harvard University, Cambridge, Massachusetts; B.A. (1880)
Attended Columbia University Law School, New York City,
New York (1880-1881)
RELIGION
Dutch Reformed
OCCUPATIONS
Rancher, writer, historian, and politician
MILITARY SERVICE
Lieutenant colonel, then colonel, First U.S. Volunteer
Cavalry Regiment (Rough Riders) (1898)
PREPRESIDENTIAL OFFICES
New York State Assemblyman (1882-1884)
U.S. Civil Service Commissioner (1889-1895)
President of New York Board of Police Commissioners
(1895-1897)
Assistant Secretary of the Navy (1897-1898)
Governor of New York (1899-1901)
Vice-President (1901)
POLITICAL PARTY
Republican, ran on Progressive ticket in 1912
INAUGURATED AS PRESIDENT
First term: September 14, 1901, Buffalo, New York
Second term: March 4, 1905, the Capitol, Washington, D.C.
AGE AT INAUGURATION
42
DIED
Oyster Bay, New York, January 6, 1919, age 60

WILLIAM HOWARD TAFT

TWENTY-SEVENTH PRESIDENT 1909-1913

As this portrait clearly indicates, the most striking characteristic of William Howard Taft's appearance was his prodigious size. Never a vain man, Taft did not mind when friends ribbed him about his girth and he frequently joked about it himself. On one occasion, after squeezing himself into a theater seat, he turned to his companion and said, "Horace, if this theater burns, it has got to burn around me."

The plate above is a souvenir from the 1908 Republican presidential campaign. Surrounding the portraits of William Howard Taft and his running mate, James S. Sherman, are images of previous Republican nominees.

In 1904, President Theodore Roosevelt appointed his close friend William Howard Taft secretary of war. Taft's role exceeded the usual functions of the post in that he also became Roosevelt's roving ambassador and trouble-shooter. Among other assignments, Taft was sent to investigate delays in the building of the Panama Canal and to keep an eye on the Philippines. The photograph above was taken in 1905 in Yokohama, Japan, where he stopped off on a return trip from the Philippines to discuss the Russo-Japanese War. Behind him is Roosevelt's daughter, Alice.

Despite his early involvement in Republican politics in his native Ohio, William Howard Taft never aspired to great political power or high elective office. Above all, he never wanted to be president. He much preferred the life of the law, and his most cherished ambition was one day to sit on the United States Supreme Court.

For many years that was exactly the goal toward which Taft seemed to be steadily moving. Appointed to fill a vacancy in the Ohio superior court in 1887, he performed so creditably that within a few years he was being mentioned as a Supreme Court possibility. His sound reputation as a state judge led to his appointment as solicitor general in Benjamin Harrison's administration. When that in turn led to a federal circuit judgeship, the fulfillment of Taft's ultimate professional ambition seemed not far off.

In 1900, however, Taft's career took a detour; William McKinley chose him to head a commission charged with quelling an insurrection in the Philippines. A year later, Taft became governor of the newly acquired territory. Then, in 1904, Theodore Roosevelt brought him home to be his secretary of war. Although Taft still yearned for the Supreme Court bench, Roosevelt's great regard and enthusiasm for him again thwarted that ambition. As the national election of 1908 neared, Roosevelt cajoled a reluctant Taft into seeking the presidential nomination, and in 1909 Taft entered the White House as Roosevelt's hand-picked successor.

In many respects, Taft's presidency was a continuation of the so-called "progressive" reform policies that Roosevelt had implemented to correct the inequities in the nation's commercial and industrial life. Under Taft the government stepped up its campaign to curb business monopolies, for example, and strengthened the regulatory powers of the Interstate Commerce Commission. But Taft had no flair for staving off critics by advertising these and other solid accomplishments of his administration. As a result, when his administration was unjustifiably accused of backsliding on the land conservation policies begun by his predecessor, Taft proved ill-equipped to defend himself. Worse yet, he was unable to allay the perception within the progressive wing of his Republican party that he had betrayed all the good work that Roosevelt had done.

Among the loudest of the progressive critics was Roosevelt himself. Consequently, soon after Taft won the Republican presidential nomination in 1912, Roosevelt launched his own campaign as the presidential candidate of the anti-Taft Republicans, who now called themselves the Progressive party. In the end, the Taft-Roosevelt split served neither man very well. Instead, it only made it easier for the Democratic candidate, Woodrow Wilson, to win in the final election.

For Taft, however, this outcome was a blessing. Having sought the presidency only because Roosevelt wanted him to, he had never really enjoyed his White House tenure. When it was over, he was greatly relieved. But Taft's public career was far from over. In 1921, he finally gained the prize he had always wanted. On October 3rd of that year, he was sworn in as chief justice of the Supreme Court.

BORN
Cincinnati, Ohio, September 15, 1857

ANCESTRY
English

WIFE
Helen (Nellie) Herron
Born: Cincinnati, Ohio
June 2, 1861
Died: Washington, D.C.
May 22, 1943

MARRIED
Cincinnati, Ohio, June 19, 1886

CHILDREN
Robert Alphonso (1889-1953)
Helen (1891-   )
Charles Phelps II (1897-1917)

EDUCATION
Yale University, New Haven, Connecticut: B.A. (1878)
Attended Cincinnati Law School, Cincinnati, Ohio
(1878-1880)

RELIGION
Unitarian

OCCUPATIONS
Reporter, lawyer, judge, and Kent Professor of
Constitutional Law at Yale University

PREPRESIDENTIAL OFFICES
Assistant Prosecuting Attorney, Hamilton County, Ohio
(1881-1882)
Collector of Internal Revenue (1882-1883)
Ohio Superior Court Judge (1887-1890)
U.S. Solicitor General (1890-1892)
Federal Circuit Court Judge (1892-1900)
Commissioner, then Governor General of the Philippines
(1901-1904)
Secretary of War (1904-1908)
Provisional Governor of Cuba (1906)

POLITICAL PARTY
Republican

INAUGURATED AS PRESIDENT
March 4, 1909, House of Representatives,
Washington, D.C

AGE AT INAUGURATION
51

POSTPRESIDENTIAL OFFICES
Joint chairman of National War Labor Board (1918)
Justice of U.S. Supreme Court (1921-1930)

DIED
Washington, D.C., March 8, 1930, age 72

WOODROW WILSON

TWENTY-EIGHTH PRESIDENT   1913–1921

Among the most frequently noted qualities that Woodrow Wilson brought to his presidency was an unrelenting faith in the correctness of his convictions that often made it difficult for him to brook disagreement with his views. Frankly admitting to this trait, Wilson himself once said, "I feel sorry for those who disagree with me." Looking at Edmund Tarbell's austerely puritanical interpretation of Wilson in this portrait, it is easy to imagine him saying that.

The signing of the Treaty of Versailles on June 28, 1919, which marked the end of World War I, is depicted in the painting below by John Christen Johansen. President Wilson believed that the treaty, once signed, would mark the beginning of a new and peaceful era founded upon the establishment of the League of Nations. Instead Wilson was bitterly disappointed when the Republican majority in the Senate refused to approve the Treaty or United States participation in the League. Nevertheless, as a result of his idealistic crusade for peace he was awarded the Nobel Peace Prize in 1919.

This poster portrays General John Joseph Pershing, commander of United States forces in Europe during World War I. It was used in 1918 in a drive to raise money for the war effort. Despite Woodrow Wilson's strong desire not to involve the United States in the European conflict, Germany's actions, especially its policy of unrestricted submarine warfare, finally forced America into the war.

When New Jersey's Democratic bosses first began hearing suggestions early in 1910 that they might do well to run Woodrow Wilson for the state governorship, a good many of them simply sneered. After all, they asked, what could this one-time college professor, who had spent his last eight years as president of Princeton University, know about the real world of rough and tumble politics? But in light of voter malaise about the rampant corruption of New Jersey's political machines, the bosses began to look more favorably on Wilson's gubernatorial candidacy. As they mulled the matter over, Wilson increasingly seemed to be tailor-made for their purposes. On the one hand, because he was good with the high-sounding phrase and free of any machine taint, he was eminently electable. On the other, because he was a political neophyte, the bosses would have no trouble controlling him once he was in office.

As governor, however, Wilson was not the mere "window dressing" his backers expected him to be. Over the strenuous objections of his party's leaders, he was soon launching an ambitious program of reform that, among other things, called for cleaning up the state's graft-ridden utility industry and a new corrupt practices law. Within a year, the New Jersey legislature had enacted virtually all of his proposals.

In the wake of this reforming whirlwind, New Jersey quickly became a model of sound state government and it was soon clear that Wilson was destined for higher things. By early 1912, a move was well underway to send him to the White House.

Once elected to the presidency, Wilson proved to be every bit as dynamic as he had been as governor. The early years of his administration brought a host of landmark reforms designed to meet the growing need for a stronger federal role in the nation's economic life. Among those measures were the establishment of a Federal Reserve System for regulating currency and banking; a strengthening of the country's antitrust laws; and legislation limiting workers on the nation's railroads to an eight-hour day.

Measured on the basis of its domestic reforms, Wilson's administration was singularly successful. But when World War I forced him into a role of international leadership, Wilson met with tragic failure. Reluctantly declaring war on Germany in 1917, Wilson brought an international idealism to his wartime leadership that called for an unvindictive peace agreement after Germany was defeated.

Unfortunately, the country's British, French, and Italian allies balked at Wilson's vision of "peace without victory." As a result, from the moment the Treaty of Versailles ending the war was signed in 1919, it was clear that in its harsh treatment of Germany the treaty had sown the seeds of another war. Wilson's only consolation was that at least the agreement contained provision for realizing one of his most cherished hopes —the establishment of an international peacekeeping organization known as the League of Nations. But even that victory became hollow when the isolationist-minded Senate refused to endorse the entry of the United States into the League. After suffering a severe stroke in the course of his public relations battle to force Senate acceptance of the League, Wilson left the White House thoroughly broken, both physically and emotionally.

BORN
Staunton, Virginia, December 28, 1856

ANCESTRY
Scottish-Irish

FIRST WIFE
Ellen Louise Axson
Born: Savannah, Georgia
May 15, 1860
Died: Washington, D.C.
August 6, 1914

SECOND WIFE
Edith Bolling Galt
Born: Wytheville, Virginia
October 15, 1872
Died: Washington, D.C.
December 18, 1961

MARRIED
First Marriage: Savannah, Georgia, June 24, 1885
Second Marriage: Washington, D.C., December 18, 1915

CHILDREN
Margaret Woodrow (1886-1944)
Jessie Woodrow (1887-1932)
Eleanor Randolph (1889-1967)

HOME
Woodrow Wilson House, 2340 S Street, N.W.,
Washington, D.C.

EDUCATION
Princeton University, Princeton, New Jersey; B.A. (1879)
Attended University of Virginia Law School,
Charlottesville, Virginia (1879-1880)
Johns Hopkins University, Baltimore Maryland; Ph.D. in
political science (1886)

RELIGION
Presbyterian

OCCUPATIONS
Lawyer, teacher, writer, and president of Princeton
University

PREPRESIDENTIAL OFFICES
Governor of New Jersey (1911-1913)

POLITICAL PARTY
Democratic

INAUGURATED AS PRESIDENT
First term: March 4, 1913, the Capitol, Washington, D.C.
Second term: March 5, 1917, the Capitol, Washington, D.C.

AGE AT INAUGURATION
56

DIED
Washington, D.C., February 3, 1924, age 67

WARREN G. HARDING

TWENTY-NINTH PRESIDENT   1921–1923

As many of his contemporaries frequently noted, Warren G. Harding's finely chiseled features and confident bearing made him look like a president. Had he been an actor, movie directors would have been knocking at his door whenever the script at hand included a statesmanlike character. But behind that impressive exterior was a man who remained forever insecure about his ability to lead. "I listen to one side and they seem right," he once remarked in connection with an issue facing his presidency, "and then—God!—I talk to the other side and they seem just as right. . . . I know somewhere there is a book that will give me the truth. But hell! I couldn't read the book."

This statue of Warren Harding's dog, Laddie Boy, was cast from the pennies donated by newsboys from across the United States in memory of the President. The idea for this commemoration was inspired by Harding's many years as the owner and publisher of the Marion, Ohio, newspaper, the Star.

Warren Harding left most executive responsibilities to the men he appointed to serve him. In the case of his secretary of state, Charles Evans Hughes, above, he chose exceptionally well. One of the most able public figures of his day, Hughes was the main spirit behind the Washington Naval Conference of 1921 that resulted in a series of treaties among the major world powers limiting the construction of warships. These agreements are often considered to be the Harding administration's most significant achievement. When Hughes resigned as secretary of state in 1925, the London Times described him as the "most compelling figure among Foreign Ministers of the post-war period."

During the first two decades of the twentieth century, the reforming administrations of Theodore Roosevelt, Woodrow Wilson, and, to some extent, William Howard Taft accustomed Americans to an aggressive presidential style that the country had rarely seen since the days of Lincoln. But by 1920, the electorate was no longer looking for a strong chief executive. In that year, voters cast their presidential lot with Republican hopeful Warren Harding, a convivial one-time newspaper editor from Ohio whose one term in the Senate had clearly demonstrated little talent for leadership and whose speeches often seemed to be words in search of ideas.

The explanation for this dramatic shift in the public's taste in White House occupants was essentially twofold. First, many Americans had simply lost their taste for progressive reform and they felt in need of some respite from presidentially inspired changes. Second, there was Harding himself, whose good-natured ways and campaign cry for a return to "normalcy" seemed to answer nicely the widespread desire for a water-treading presidency.

In many respects that was the type of administration that Harding actually gave the country. A man of slight intellect, who much preferred the camaraderie of the golf course and the poker table to the world of serious critical thought, Harding allowed the nation to enjoy itself.

His presidency was not without substantial accomplishments. To a large extent, however, its achievements were primarily due to members of his cabinet rather than to Harding himself. On the recommendation of Andrew Mellon, his secretary of the treasury, for example, Congress established a Budget Bureau, which promised to bring new efficiency to the task of allocating federal spending. Similarly, it was Harding's secretary of commerce, Herbert Hoover, who took the initiative in transforming the Commerce Department from a political backwater into a major clearinghouse for the nation's economic data.

Although some of Harding's advisers served him and the country well, others within his presidential circle did not. For Harding had included in his administration a number of men who obtained their positions not because they were capable, but because they were his friends. Unfortunately, honesty was not among the stronger attributes of some of these men. The result was public corruption on a grand scale. While Harding's Veterans' Bureau director, Charles Forbes, disposed of army surplus supplies in exchange for bribes, his secretary of the interior, Albert Fall, was trading leases on government oil lands for handsome deposits in his own bank account. Meanwhile, Jesse Smith, the longtime crony of Attorney General Harry Daugherty, was engaged in selling immunity from prosecution to violators of the country's new Prohibition law.

Harding, however, never had to face the full consequences of these and other scandals in his administration. In June 1923, seeking to escape the anxieties caused by mounting evidence of his friends' wrongdoing, he set out on a tour of the West. Several weeks later he was dead from causes that were not entirely clear, but that were undoubtedly related to a general deterioration of his circulatory system.

BORN
Bloomington Grove, Ohio, November 2, 1865

ANCESTRY
English-Dutch and Scottish-Irish

WIFE
Florence Kling De Wolfe
Born: Marion, Ohio
August 15, 1860
Died: Marion, Ohio
November 21, 1924

MARRIED
Marion, Ohio, July 8, 1891

CHILDREN
None

HOME
380 Mount Vernon Avenue, Marion, Ohio

EDUCATION
Ohio Central College, Iberia, Ohio; B.S. (1882)

RELIGION
Baptist

OCCUPATIONS
Newspaper editor and publisher

PREPRESIDENTIAL OFFICES
Member of the Ohio Senate (1899-1903)
Lieutenant Governor of Ohio (1904-1905)
Member of the U.S. Senate (1915-1921)

POLITICAL PARTY
Republican

INAUGURATED AS PRESIDENT
March 4, 1921, the Capitol, Washington D.C.

AGE AT INAUGURATION
55

DIED
San Francisco, California, August 2, 1923, age 57

CALVIN COOLIDGE

THIRTIETH PRESIDENT 1923–1929

When Ercole Cartotto painted the original version of this portrait in 1928 for Calvin Coolidge's college fraternity, he intended to portray the president as a "man absorbed by duty and steeled by responsibility." There is, indeed, a sense of sober earnestness about the picture. But others regarded the likeness in a more humorous light. In describing it, one reporter said that Coolidge looked "as if, without further provocation, he would bite the person or persons unknown who obviously had been annoying him."

On the morning of May 20, 1927, twenty-five-year-old Charles A. Lindbergh took off from New York in his monoplane, the Spirit of St. Louis. *When he landed thirty-three and a half hours later at Le Bourget Airport outside Paris, he had completed the first nonstop solo flight across the Atlantic and had become an international celebrity. It was a testament to the great excitement engendered by this feat that even the normally reticent Calvin Coolidge greeted the young pilot on his return to the United States with an "unrestrained cordiality" rarely seen during his presidency.*

Of all the men pictured in this group photograph of Coolidge and his first cabinet, Coolidge was perhaps the most disengaged from both the daily workings and the long-range policy-making of his administration. Once when Secretary of Labor James J. Davis sent him papers on a matter which Davis thought required presidential attention, Coolidge sent the papers back and said, "You tell ol' man Davis I hired him as Secretary of Labor and if he can't do the job I'll get a new Secretary of Labor."

"In politics, one must meet people and that's not easy for me. . . . When I was a little fellow . . . the hardest thing in the world was to go through the kitchen door and give [strangers] a welcome. . . . I'm all right with old friends, but every time I meet a stranger I've got to go through the old kitchen door . . . and it's not easy." So Calvin Coolidge once described his feelings when it came to performing the most fundamental task of politics. But not only did he find this task difficult; he also never managed, and perhaps did not even try, to conceal that fact very well.

Thus, when he came to Washington in 1921 as Warren Harding's vice-president, observers were frankly taken aback by this "well of silence" that now occupied the nation's second-highest office. Soon stories regarding his unwillingness to converse were legion. Among the most widely circulated was one told about a Washington socialite who bet a friend that she would get "Silent Cal" to say more than three words to her. After several failed attempts, she finally informed Coolidge of the wager. To which he responded, "You lose."

But, despite his aloofness, somehow Coolidge had managed to make his way in the political world, rising from unpaid councilman in Northampton, Massachusetts, to the Massachusetts governorship and, finally, to the vice-presidency. Then, in 1923, with the unexpected death of Harding, he succeeded to the White House.

Calvin Coolidge proved to be a widely popular chief executive and, in the election of 1924, he claimed the presidency in his own right by a substantial popular majority. To a large degree, Coolidge's popularity derived from his conservative unwillingness to use the powers of his office to monitor the workings of the economy. "The business of America," he once declared, "is business," indicating that the wisest strategy for his administration was to give free rein to the country's commercial and industrial genius. In an era marked by unparalleled prosperity, this passive outlook seemed to suit the nation's needs perfectly. As the economic boom reached undreamed of heights during his presidency, "Coolidge prosperity" became a catch phrase suggesting that the days of a rising and falling business cycle were past.

Part of Coolidge's appeal lay in his reticent personality. When combined with his reputation for honesty and his stoic New England habits, this diffidence represented for many a reassuring antidote to the corruption of the Harding administration and to the uninhibited self-indulgence that accompanied the boom of the twenties.

Unfortunately, the days of "Coolidge prosperity" were numbered. Although Coolidge himself refused to see it, beneath the appearance of good times were serious weaknesses in the economic structure of the United States. In late 1929, the collapse of the stock market marked the onset of the most serious depression that the country had ever experienced. By then, however, Coolidge was out of office, and blame for this disaster went to his successor.

BORN
Plymouth Notch, Vermont, July 4, 1872

ANCESTRY
English

WIFE
Grace Anna Goodhue
Born: Burlington, Vermont
January 3, 1879
Died: Northampton, Massachusetts
July 8, 1957

MARRIED
Burlington, Vermont, October 4, 1905

CHILDREN
John (1906-   )
Calvin (1908-1924)

HOME
Coolidge Homestead, Plymouth, Vermont

EDUCATION
Amherst College, Amherst, Massachusetts; B.A. (1895)

RELIGION
Congregationalist

OCCUPATIONS
Lawyer, politician, and writer

PREPRESIDENTIAL OFFICES
Member of the Massachusetts House of Representatives
(1907-1908)
Mayor of Northampton, Massachusetts (1910-1911)
Member and President of Massachusetts Senate (1912-1915)
Lieutenant Governor of Massachusetts (1916-1918)
Governor of Massachusetts (1919-1920)
Vice-President (1921-1923)

POLITICAL PARTY
Republican

INAUGURATED AS PRESIDENT
First term: August 3, 1923, Plymouth Notch, Vermont
Second term: March 4, 1925, the Capitol, Washington, D.C.

AGE AT INAUGURATION
51

DIED
Northampton, Massachusetts, January 5, 1933, age 60

HERBERT HOOVER

THIRTY-FIRST PRESIDENT   1929–1933

A prodigiously hard worker, Herbert Hoover did not always have much patience with portraitists. While heading the country's Food Administrations during World War I, for example, he only grudgingly admitted one artist into his office and then proceeded to work at his desk without ever once looking in the artist's direction. When painting this portrait in 1931, however, Douglas Chandor was more fortunate. Although initially "abstracted" by his presidential cares, Hoover finally warmed to Chandor and, in the process, shed some of the remoteness that characterized his presidential leadership.

Democratic candidate Alfred E. Smith had almost no chance to win the presidential election of 1928 against Republican Herbert Hoover, primarily because the nation was enjoying an era of great prosperity and was unwilling to vote out the Republicans who claimed responsibility for it. In addition, Smith was of Irish-Catholic origin and in the view of many Protestant voters this automatically disqualified him for the country's highest office.

Herbert Hoover's rigid faith in the principles of a free market economy made it impossible for him to institute massive federal programs to ease the Great Depression that set in during his presidency. One of the few measures that he did implement was the Reconstruction Finance Corporation, which provided loans mainly to big business. But when it came to Federal sponsorship of outright relief for the unemployed, he drew the line in the belief that such "handouts" would destroy the nation's private initiative. Hoover's deeply rooted conservatism also prevented him from taking a role in helping labor unions to promote the interests of their members. His administration, therefore, never considered it appropriate to interfere in such incidents as the Mountaineer Coal Company strike where management ultimately defeated its workers' demands by bringing in the "breaker boys," pictured here.

If ever there was a man who seemed able to make a success of the presidency, it was Herbert Hoover. By the time he entered the White House in March 1929, his past achievements were a study in laudatory superlatives. As a mining engineer, he had enjoyed an international reputation as the "doctor of sick mines" and, by the age of forty, his ability to transform marginal ore-extracting operations into thriving enterprises had made this once-impoverished orphan a multimillionaire. During World War I, he turned his energies to feeding the civilian populations of war-ravaged Europe and, after the United States entered the war, to serving as the country's chief food administrator. Once again his ability to deal effectively with the tasks at hand was superb. By the end of the war, his work in supplying food to Europe's starving populations had earned him the sobriquet "The Great Humanitarian." The list of Hoover's accomplishments, however, did not stop there. As secretary of commerce under presidents Harding and Coolidge, he applied to his department much the same magic he had once applied to ailing mines. He changed the Department of Commerce from a comfortable sinecure for political hacks to a dynamic information clearinghouse for all phases of business and industry.

If Hoover's personal credentials boded well for his presidency, so, too, did the times. With the stock market moving ever upward and much of the nation enjoying a record prosperity, it seemed to many that Hoover's campaign assertion that he and his Republican party were about to banish the poorhouse from America forever was not merely an idle promise.

Seven months after Hoover took office, however, the rosy prospects for his presidency acquired a decidedly gloomy tinge. With the great stock market crash in the autumn of 1929, the curtain suddenly came down on the boom prosperity of the late 1920s, and the nation began its plunge into the deepest and most painful depression in its history.

In responding to this disaster, Hoover operated on a conservative faith that the country's strength lay in its "rugged individualism" and that the real solution for relieving the sufferings of the swelling ranks of unemployed must come from the private sector. He therefore flatly rejected proposals for massive federal works projects as a means of alleviating unemployment and was even more opposed to any kind of federally funded welfare relief. Hoover believed that his administration could do little to halt the Great Depression. When worsening conditions belatedly prompted him to depart from these views by implementing programs for channeling loans to the country's failing businesses and farmers, their impact was woefully limited.

Not surprisingly, Hoover's reluctance to act effectively had a dimming effect on his once lustrous reputation. But inactivity was not the only tarnishing agent at work; equally damaging was Hoover's coldly businesslike presidential style, which made it seem that The Great Humanitarian, who had rushed to the aid of starving Europe during World War I, simply did not care about the misfortunes of his fellow Americans. By the time Hoover left office in 1933, he had become one of the most maligned presidents in the history of the United States.

BORN
West Branch, Iowa, August 10, 1874

ANCESTRY
Swiss-German

WIFE
Lou Henry
Born: Waterloo, Iowa
March 29, 1874
Died: New York City, New York
January 7, 1944

MARRIED
Monterey, California, February 10, 1899

CHILDREN
Herbert Clark (1903-1969)
Allan Henry (1907-)

HOME
Herbert Hoover Birthplace, West Branch, Iowa

EDUCATION
Stanford University, Stanford, California; B.A. (1895)

RELIGION
Quaker

OCCUPATIONS
Engineer and writer

PREPRESIDENTIAL OFFICES
Chairman of the Commission for Relief in Belgium
(1917-1918)
U.S. Food Administrator (1917-1919)
Chairman of the Supreme Economic Council (1919-1920)
Secretary of Commerce (1921-1928)

POLITICAL PARTY
Republican

INAUGURATED AS PRESIDENT
March 4, 1929, the Capitol, Washington, D.C.

AGE AT INAUGURATION
54

POSTPRESIDENTIAL OFFICES
Chairman of Commission for Polish Relief (1939)
Chairman of Finnish Relief Fund (1939)
Coordinator of Food Supply for World Famine (1946-1947)
Chairman of commissions on Organization of the Executive
Branch of Government (1947-1949)
Commission on Government Operations (1953-1955)

DIED
New York City, New York, October 20, 1964, age 90

FRANKLIN D. ROOSEVELT

THIRTY-SECOND PRESIDENT   1933–1945

This portrait of Franklin D. Roosevelt by Douglas Chandor was never meant to be a formal likeness. Rather, it is a study for the never-completed larger composition that the artist sketched in miniature in the picture's lower left corner, showing Roosevelt with his wartime allies, Winston Churchill and Joseph Stalin, at the Yalta Conference. Roosevelt had just come back from that meeting when he posed for Chandor, and he was looking worn and haggard. The artist, however, chose to portray his presidential subject in a light that suggested far greater vigor than reality warranted.

When Franklin Roosevelt became president in March 1933, his wife, Eleanor, entered the White House declaring that she was "just going to be plain, ordinary Mrs. Roosevelt. And that's all." That promise, however, was not long kept. Driven by her own keen sensitivity to human suffering and social justice, Eleanor Roosevelt soon became almost as engrossed in the politics of the new administration as were her husband's official advisers. Touring the nation's economically distressed communities, she returned to Washington prepared to encourage federally sponsored planned communities. She also made speeches and gave press conferences where she spoke her mind on such issues as child labor. Perhaps most important, she acted as her husband's conscience, urging him toward various reforms that he might otherwise have avoided in the name of expedience. As she herself put it shortly after FDR's death, "I think I sometimes acted as a spur even though the spurring was not always welcome." This photograph of Mrs. Roosevelt was taken in 1944, when she was sixty years old.

The prohibition of alcoholic beverages in the United States at the close of World War I gave rise to illicit trade in spirits and became a major cause of crime and corruption. In 1932, the repeal of Prohibition became a Democratic pledge and on December 5, 1933, the "great experiment" in enforced temperance was ended.

Raised in a sheltered world of wealth and social privilege, Franklin Roosevelt did not exhibit much drive in his youth, and he seemed marked for a life of genteel ease in which his main preoccupations would be sitting on corporate boards and looking after his family's investments. By about 1907, however, when his distant cousin Theodore Roosevelt was in the White House, the young patrician began to entertain ambitions of quite a different kind. While chatting idly one day with his fellow clerks at a prestigious New York law firm, he outlined a plan for making his way in politics that strongly resembled the path that Teddy Roosevelt had traveled and that "with any luck," he claimed, would take him, too, to the presidency.

What had seemed a youthful boast became a spectacular reality. By 1929, despite a crippling bout with polio, Franklin Roosevelt had indeed—like Cousin Theodore before him—gone from a seat in the New York legislature to a tenure as assistant secretary of the navy and was ensconced in the New York governorship. Four years later, as the United States sank ever deeper into the Great Depression, he took the presidential oath of office.

So began one of the most remarkable presidencies in American history. Coming to office against a backdrop of hopelessness and suffering, Roosevelt brought with him a reassuring warmth and compassion that seemed to engender optimism from the first day of his administration. More important, he brought a zest for innovation that was to redefine the federal government's role in American life. Before long his New Deal administration was implementing a myriad of depression-healing measures that left no phase of the country's economy untouched. For the unemployed, there were public works projects. For farmers, there were programs to bolster commodity prices. For the nation's collapsing banking system, there was a plan for protecting bank deposits, and for the securities market, there were new regulations to curb the irresponsible speculation that had been one of the root causes of the depression.

In implementing these and the host of other measures that made up his New Deal, Roosevelt was not entirely successful in reviving the economy, and he drew bitter criticism from conservatives who saw his policies as first steps on the road to communism. But for the vast majority of Americans, he was a savior, and when Roosevelt took the unprecedented step in 1940 of seeking a third presidential term, he could not be denied.

By then, however, Roosevelt's concerns had shifted focus. With Nazi Germany overrunning Europe and Japan seeking hegemony in the Far East, it was becoming clear that sooner or later the United States would be embroiled in war. Finally, the inevitable happened and, following the Japanese attack on Pearl Harbor, Hawaii, on December 7, 1941, Roosevelt faced the task of leading the country through World War II.

In shouldering that responsibility, Roosevelt paid a heavy personal price. Over the next several years his health greatly deteriorated. He died shortly after his election to a fourth term, just as the United States and its allies were about to triumph over Germany and Japan.

BORN
Hyde Park, New York, January 30, 1882

ANCESTRY
Dutch and French-Hugenot

WIFE
Anna Eleanor Roosevelt
Born: New York City, New York
October 11, 1884
Died: New York City, New York
November 7, 1962

MARRIED
New York City, New York, March 17, 1905

CHILDREN
Anna Eleanor (1906-1975)
James (1907-   )
Elliott (1910-1990)
Franklin Delano, Jr. (1914-1988)
John Aspinwall (1916-1981)

HOME
Hyde Park, New York

EDUCATION
Harvard University, Cambridge, Massachusetts; B.A. (1903)
Studied at Columbia University Law School, New York City,
New York (1904-1907)

RELIGION
Episcopalian

OCCUPATIONS
Lawyer and politician

PREPRESIDENTIAL OFFICES
Member of the New York State Senate (1911-1913)
Assistant Secretary of the Navy (1913-1920)
Governor of New York (1929-1933)

POLITICAL PARTY
Democratic

INAUGURATED AS PRESIDENT
First term: March 4, 1933, the Capitol, Washington, D.C.
Second term: January 20, 1937, the Capitol,
Washington, D.C.
Third term: January 20, 1941, the Capitol,
Washington, D.C.
Fourth term: January 20, 1945, south portico of
the White House, Washington, D.C.

AGE AT INAUGURATION
51

DIED
Warm Springs, Georgia, April 12, 1945, age 63

HARRY S TRUMAN

THIRTY-THIRD PRESIDENT 1945–1953

Harry S Truman's formal education stopped at high school. But his appetite for learning remained voracious throughout his life, and he rarely passed up an opportunity to expand his knowledge. When he posed for this likeness by Greta Kempton in 1948, he made it the occasion for improving his knowledge of art and, according to Kempton, much of the conversation with her presidential subject consisted of questions and answers about the techniques of painting a portrait.

Early in 1945, Vice-President Harry Truman attended a National Press Club party where, much to his wife's disapproval, he was photographed playing a piano with actress Lauren Bacall seductively perched on its top. The picture became the inspiration for this caricature of Truman and his Republican opponent, Thomas E. Dewey, during the presidential campaign of 1948. It was done by Ben Shahn, who had little use for either man.

When Franklin Roosevelt died during the closing days of World War II, it fell to Truman to end the war and formulate policies for a new world order. Among his chief advisers in these matters were the four men pictured here with Truman, left to right: Chairman of the Joint Chiefs of Staff Admiral William D. Leahy; Army Air Force General Henry H. Arnold; Army Chief of Staff George C. Marshall; and Navy Commander in Chief Ernest J. King. Arnold and King retired to private life shortly after the war ended. Marshall eventually became Truman's secretary of state and a chief formulator of the hugely successful Marshall Plan for rebuilding war-torn western Europe. Leahy, who remained in Truman's administration until 1949, was prominent among those who urged Truman to take a strong stand against the Soviet Union's postwar efforts to extend its influence in Europe and Asia.

There is an epitaph in Boot Hill cemetery in Arizona which reads, 'Here lies Jack Williams. He done his damnedest! What more can a person do?' Well, that's all I could do. I did my damnedest, and that's all there was to it!" That is how Harry Truman summed up his presidency shortly after leaving the White House in 1953.

The peppery, plain-spoken Truman had never wanted to be president. A one-time haberdasher who by 1936 had risen through the state Democratic machine to a seat in the Senate, he was quite satisfied with being a senator, and he had agreed only reluctantly in 1944 to serve as Franklin Roosevelt's vice-presidential running mate. His reluctance soon turned to fear as Truman realized that the gravely ill Roosevelt probably would not survive four more years in the White House and that at some point he would himself almost certainly be president. That point came sooner than expected. On April 12, 1945, less than three months after his inauguration, Roosevelt died. A dazed Truman girded himself for the tasks of leading the country through the final phases of World War II and overseeing its postwar adjustments to peace. Among his first and most difficult decisions was to order the dropping of the newly developed atomic bomb on Hiroshima and Nagasaki, thus ushering in the nuclear era.

Eventually, Truman came to relish the presidency, but enjoyment of the office did not always bring success. Throughout his eight years in the White House, his relations with Congress were rocky at best, and his visionary Fair Deal, which called for such things as national medical insurance and strong civil rights legislation, generally received a cold shoulder in the House even from many of his Democratic allies. Also on the negative side was Truman's sometimes stubborn loyalty to a network of political cronies who had few scruples about using influence within the administration for private gain.

Despite whiffs of scandal and difficulties with Congress, Truman could nevertheless claim some significant achievements. In the face of the Soviet Union's postwar drive to expand communist influence westward in Europe, for example, it was the aggressive implementation of his so-called "Truman Doctrine" of containment that largely put an end to this disturbing development and led to the formation of NATO and the beginning of the Cold War. Also much to Truman's credit was the Marshall Plan for rejuvenating Western Europe's ravaged economies after World War II through massive infusions of United States aid. Named for Secretary of State George Marshall, the plan eventually became one of the most singular diplomatic triumphs in United States history.

By the end of his presidency, Truman's inability to end a war against communist aggression in Korea, combined with his continued bickering with Congress and allegations that his administration harbored communist infiltrators, made him seem an incompetent fumbler. Gradually, however, that perception changed. By the time Truman died in 1972, it was widely conceded that he had indeed "done his damnedest" and that his damnedest had actually been pretty good.

BORN
Lamar, Missouri, May 8, 1884

ANCESTRY
English-Scottish-Irish

WIFE
Elizabeth Virginia (Bess) Wallace
Born: Independence Missouri
February 13, 1885
Died: Independence, Missouri
October 18, 1982

MARRIED
Independence, Missouri, June 28, 1919

CHILDREN
Margaret (1924-   )

EDUCATION
Attended Kansas City School of Law, Kansas City, Missouri
(1923-1925)

RELIGION
Baptist

OCCUPATIONS
Railroad timekeeper, bank clerk, farmer, haberdasher,
politician, and judge

MILITARY SERVICE
Missouri National Guard (1905-1911)
Rose from first lieutenant to major, 129th Field Artillery
(1918-1919)

PREPRESIDENTIAL OFFICES
County Judge, Eastern District of Jackson County, Missouri
(1922-1924)
Presiding Judge, County Court, Jackson County, Missouri
(1926-1934)
Member of the U.S. Senate (1935-1945)
Vice-President (1945)

POLITICAL PARTY
Democratic

INAUGURATED AS PRESIDENT
First term: April 12, 1945, Cabinet Room of
the White House, Washington, D.C.
Second term: January 20, 1949, the Capitol,
Washington, D.C.

AGE AT INAUGURATION
60

DIED
Kansas City, Missouri, December 26, 1972, age 88

DWIGHT D. EISENHOWER

THIRTY-FOURTH PRESIDENT   1953–1961

At some point when posing for this portrait by Thomas Stephens, Dwight D. Eisenhower became fascinated with the mysteries of painting. After studying Stephens's technique for a while, he suddenly exclaimed, "By golly, I'd like to try that!" Ready for a break anyway, Stephens handed him a palette and brushes, and soon Eisenhower was at work on a likeness of Mrs. Eisenhower. The results of this maiden venture into picture-making were far from discouraging. Shortly thereafter Eisenhower took up painting as a hobby.

During the second term of Dwight D. Eisenhower's presidency, Alaska and Hawaii were admitted to the Union. The stamps above were released by the United States Post Office to commemorate the twenty-fifth anniversary of the forty-ninth and fiftieth states.

Although an inexperienced politician, Eisenhower's status as national military hero, his personal magnetism, his infectious grin, and a straightforward and instantly memorable slogan—shown on the campaign button right—made his election to the presidency almost assured.

During his West Point years, football was Eisenhower's favorite sport, but a knee injury forced him to give up the game. Later in life he became an avid golfer. In the 1954 photograph here, he is seen greeting his five-year-old grandson, David, during a golfing vacation in Georgia. Eisenhower's enthusiasm for golf led to the building of a putting green and driving range on the White House grounds and sometimes inspired accusations that he was not paying sufficient attention to his presidential duties.

The enormous attraction of American voters to military heroes in presidential elections had been well demonstrated by the time the United States entered World War II. As the country geared up for war with Germany and Japan, it therefore required no great political wisdom to realize that, assuming victory, this conflict would almost certainly yield an irresistibly alluring gold-braided presidential candidate. For a while it appeared that the battlefield luminary destined for a White House candidacy was Southwest Pacific commander General Douglas MacArthur. But by war's end, MacArthur had been eclipsed, and the soldier-hero who promised to be the most likely presidential contender was Dwight D. Eisenhower, the general who had orchestrated the Allied invasion of Europe.

Known affectionately as "Ike," Eisenhower had many vote-getting assets, not least of which were his broad grin and warm, fatherly manner. But before those assets could be made to work their magic in a presidential election, one stumbling block had to be surmounted: Eisenhower did not want to be president, and in 1948, in the face of efforts to make him a presidential candidate, he flatly declared that a professional soldier had no business going into politics. Over the next several years, however, his views changed, and in 1953, following a landslide victory at the polls, Eisenhower was assuming the office he had once so emphatically rejected.

After Eisenhower left the White House in 1961, a good many people believed that he had not been a particularly successful president. To substantiate that judgment, they often cited his unwillingness to denounce Senator Joseph McCarthy's divisive and groundless campaign to uncover communist traitors in the government and his reluctance to use his presidential prestige to gain compliance with the Supreme Court's 1954 mandate for desegregating the nation's public schools. Some also claimed that in responding to the Cold War and Sino-Soviet efforts to expand communist influence in the world, Eisenhower added unnecessarily to international tensions by too often resorting to military confrontation to block those efforts.

But there was a side to Eisenhower's administration that, as the years passed, increasingly cast his presidency in a more positive light, even among some former critics. As a fiscal conservative, for example, Eisenhower assiduously insisted on maintaining as much as possible a balanced federal budget and, in doing so, provided a favorable climate for the nation's steady economic growth during his two terms in the White House. Moreover, although he often favored armed intervention to halt communism's spread in various parts of the globe, he understood the limits of that strategy. Knowing that such saber-rattling diplomacy could one day spark an all-out nuclear war, he made it his business to explore less warlike means for achieving peaceful coexistence between the American-led free world and the Soviet-led communist world. In the short term, those explorations yielded little of substance. Nevertheless, through his meetings with Soviet leader Nikita Khrushchev and his proposals for international disarmament, Eisenhower could be credited with paving the way for thaws in the Cold War.

BORN
Denison, Texas, October 14, 1890

ANCESTRY
Swiss-German

WIFE
Marie (Mamie) Geneva Doud
Born: Boone, Iowa
November 14, 1896
Died: Gettysburg, Pennsylvania
November 11, 1979

MARRIED
Denver, Colorado, July 1, 1916

CHILDREN
Doud Dwight (1917-1921)
John Sheldon (1922-   )

EDUCATION
U.S. Military Academy, West Point, New York; B.S. (1915)

RELIGION
Presbyterian

OCCUPATIONS
Soldier, president of Columbia University, and writer

MILITARY SERVICE
Commissioned 2nd lieutenant, U.S. Army (1915)
Served in various posts in United States, Panama,
and Philippines (1915-1942)
Named commander of European Theater of Operations
(1942)
Named Supreme Commander of Allied Expeditionary Force
in Western Europe (1943)
Promoted to General of the Army (1944)
Named United States Army chief of staff (1945-1948)
Supreme commander of North Atlantic Treaty Organization
(1951-1952)

POLITICAL PARTY
Republican

INAUGURATED AS PRESIDENT
First term: January 20, 1953, east portico of
the White House, Washington, D.C.
Second term: January 21, 1957, the Capitol,
Washington, D.C.

AGE AT INAUGURATION
62

DIED
Washington, D.C., March 28, 1969, age 78

JOHN F. KENNEDY

The youthful vitality evident in this portrait by William Draper was the most striking characteristic of John F. Kennedy's appearance. But Kennedy's health was never as robust as it seemed. Among his recurring ailments was serious difficulty with his back that had begun with a football injury at Harvard and had substantially worsened when the PT boat he was commanding in the Pacific during World War II was shot out from under him. The severe pain resulting from these two misfortunes plagued Kennedy for the rest of his life. But even when it became close to unbearable, few were ever aware of it.

This photograph, taken at John F. Kennedy's funeral, showing his widow, Jacqueline, leading their children down the steps of the Capitol, poignantly underscored the twofold nature of the tragedy of his assassination. While the nation had lost a dynamic leader, his handsome, vibrant family had suffered an irreplaceable personal loss as well.

If Kennedy's presidency was often called Camelot, Jacqueline Kennedy was its Guinevere. With her youthful energy, beauty, and talent, she served as a role model to young women coming of age in the 1960s. In a tangible way she embodied the appeal of the Kennedy administration. She was the most popular First Lady in recent memory and regularly upstaged the president, who often joked about it.

On November 22, 1963, President John F. Kennedy arrived in Dallas, Texas, to mend political fences within his Democratic party. With the late fall sun shining brightly down on his motorcade, and his vivacious wife seated next to him in their open car, the stage seemed to be particularly well set for the success of that mission. But the optimism of the moment was soon shattered as shots rang out and Kennedy suddenly slumped over. Within seconds his presidential car was racing toward a nearby hospital where shortly after its arrival Kennedy was pronounced dead.

Kennedy's assassination plunged the nation into a deep and profound grief not experienced since the death of Lincoln nearly a century before. And along with the grief came another phenomenon that harkened back to Lincoln's martyrdom. In the months following the Dallas tragedy, the public came to see Kennedy in increasingly idealized terms, and as his virtues became ever magnified in the popular imagination, his failings seemed to fade into insignificance.

The second-youngest individual to occupy the White House, he had come to office with a cocky and sometimes naive self-assurance that he and his advisers could do anything they set their minds to. But he quickly found that this was not the case. In giving the go-ahead, for example, to the utterly disastrous Bay of Pigs invasion of Cuba to overthrow communist leader Fidel Castro in 1961, Kennedy had to accept responsibility for one of the country's most humiliating defeats in the history of the Cold War. At the same time, he had not proven particularly effective in dealing with Congress. As a result, his calls for, among other things, a far-reaching civil rights law, greater federal aid to education, and a national health care program for the elderly failed to evoke a positive response.

But Kennedy had his successes as well. When the Soviet Union threatened the United States' security by installing missiles in Cuba in 1962, he quickly undertook to impose a naval blockade on Cuba and in the process forced the removal of the missiles. His administration also reached an agreement with the Soviet Union and Great Britain that promised to put an end to most nuclear testing. Finally, although Kennedy did not succeed in convincing Congress to enact most of his domestic programs, his dynamic leadership nevertheless helped to create a climate favorable to their eventual passage under his successor, Lyndon Johnson. Nowhere was this more apparent than in the area of civil rights, and there is little doubt Kennedy's aggressive support for the struggle against racial discrimination was a major factor leading to the landmark Civil Rights Act of 1964.

The most positive aspect of Kennedy's presidency was not to be found in diplomatic agreements or new legislation. Rather, it lay in Kennedy's personal style. A man of enormous charm and wit, he injected the presidency with a cosmopolitan glamor that even his many critics found appealing. Perhaps more significant, however, was Kennedy's idealism, which, in tandem with his uncommon ability to articulate that idealism, often made it seem that a more equitable and peaceful world was indeed possible. Thus, as the Kennedy legend grew to heroic proportions after his assassination, it was not what he had done that explained this, but rather the promise of what he might have done had he lived.

BORN
Brookline, Massachusetts, May 29, 1917

ANCESTRY
Irish

WIFE
Jacqueline Lee Bouvier
Born: Southampton, New York
July 28, 1929

MARRIED
Newport, Rhode Island, September 12, 1953

CHILDREN
Caroline Bouvier (1957-   )
John Fitzgerald (1960-   )
Patrick Bouvier (1963-1963)

EDUCATION
Harvard University: B.S. (1940)
Attended Stanford University Graduate School of Business
Administration, Stanford, California (1940-1941)

RELIGION
Roman Catholic

OCCUPATIONS
Reporter, author, and politician

MILITARY SERVICE
Rose from ensign to lieutenant, U.S. Navy (1941-1945)

PREPRESIDENTIAL OFFICES
Member of the U.S. House of Representatives (1947-1953)
Member of the U.S. Senate (1953-1960)

POLITICAL PARTY
Democratic

INAUGURATED AS PRESIDENT
January 20, 1961, the Capitol, Washington, D.C.

AGE AT INAUGURATION
43

DIED
Dallas, Texas, November 22, 1963, age 46

LYNDON B. JOHNSON

THIRTY-SIXTH PRESIDENT   1963–1969

In 1964, in recognition of Lyndon B. Johnson's great success during his first year in the presidency, Time magazine designated him its Man of the Year and dispatched Peter Hurd, the noted southwestern artist, to the White House to paint his Man of the Year portrait. Johnson liked the Time likeness so much that he decided that Hurd should paint his official likeness. The result was the portrait shown here, but when Hurd unveiled it at a private presidential showing, Johnson unequivocally declared it "the ugliest thing I ever saw." Shortly thereafter the pun started making the rounds in Washington that "artists should be seen around the White House—but not Hurd."

The headline on the front page of the Washington Post, and newspapers all over the country, heralded the passage of the Civil Rights Act of 1964. Due largely to Lyndon Johnson's legislative skills, the bill was passed with a rare display of bipartisan support in the Congress and was one of the most dramatic achievements of Johnson's first year in office.

In the 1964 presidential campaign, Johnson's platform focused on continuing the policies of the Kennedy administration.

As Senator, Vice-President, and, finally, as President, Lyndon Johnson ardently promoted American space technology. In 1961, he prodded John F. Kennedy to announce the country's commitment to putting a man on the moon within a decade. In the photograph here, Johnson arrives at Cape Canaveral (then Cape Kennedy) in July 1969 to witness the launching of the manned Apollo 11 rocket whose trip into space would mark the realization of that goal.

His critics found him abrasively crude and ruthless, and even his friends had to admit that on occasion there was more than a grain of truth in that unflattering characterization. Nevertheless, there was one compliment that neither ally nor foe could deny him: No one understood the mechanisms of American politics better than Lyndon B. Johnson, and no one could use those mechanisms to more effective advantage.

Having entered the political arena as a member of the House of Representatives in 1937, this tall, broad-shouldered Texas Democrat had by the mid-1950s become the majority leader of the Senate. More important, Johnson's mastery of the arts of political arm-twisting and flattery had made him one of the most formidable figures in Washington. It was universally acknowledged by Democrats and Republicans alike that no measure of consequence could pass through Congress without his blessing.

But Johnson's ascendance in Washington came temporarily to an end in 1961 when he became John F. Kennedy's vice-president and, like all the holders of that office before him, he found himself suddenly relegated to the nation's political backwaters. In speaking of his term in the vice-presidency, he once remarked, "I detested every minute of it."

Johnson's unhappiness did not, however, erode his instincts for leadership and, when Kennedy's assassination placed him in the White House in 1963, it almost seemed that his time in vice-presidential limbo had increased his capacity for dominating. Thus, as Johnson brought his skills in political orchestration to bear on his presidential duties, he seemed to be almost infallible. By late 1965, his administration had pushed through Congress a body of legislation that could only be described as breathtaking. Perhaps the most notable of these measures was a far-reaching civil rights act, which held the promise of finally putting an end to racial discrimination in American life. But there were other significant measures as well, among them federal health insurance for the elderly, generous funding for a "war on poverty," and the most comprehensive package of federal aid to education ever enacted.

The ultimate goal of all these domestic programs, Johnson said, was the creation of a "Great Society" in which all Americans, regardless of race or birth, would be guaranteed a reasonable opportunity to share in the enormous richness of their country's resources. To a great extent, Americans shared in that dream, and for a while Johnson's approval rating in the polls was running high. But, even as his popularity soared, his commitment to protecting South Vietnam from a communist takeover planted the seeds of his political destruction. In response to his administration's rapid buildup of American forces in Vietnam after 1965, public sentiment toward Johnson increasingly soured. Meanwhile, the costliness of his "Great Society" legislation and the failure of his civil rights policies to work their desired change as rapidly as some had hoped were also diminishing his reputation. While opponents of the Vietnam War vilified him for dragging the country into a war that was neither winnable nor justifiable, others accused him of fiscal irresponsibility and trafficking in false promises. Thus, by the end of his presidency, Johnson had gone from one of the most widely approved presidents of the twentieth century to one of the most disliked. He decided not to seek reelection.

BORN
Near Stonewall, Texas, August 27, 1908

ANCESTRY
English

WIFE
Claudia Alta (Ladybird) Taylor
Born: Karnack, Texas
December 12, 1912

MARRIED
San Antonio, Texas, November 17, 1934

CHILDREN
Lydia Bird (1944-   )
Luci Baines (1947-   )

HOME
LBJ Ranch, Texas

EDUCATION
Southwest Texas State Teachers College, San Marcos, Texas;
B.S. (1930)
Attended Georgetown University Law School,
Washington, D.C. (1934)

RELIGION
Disciples of Christ

OCCUPATIONS
Teacher, rancher and politician

MILITARY SERVICE
Rose from lieutenant commander to commander, U.S. Navy
(1941-1942)

PREPRESIDENTIAL OFFICES
National Youth Administration Director in Texas
(1935-1937)
Member of the U.S. House of Representatives (1937-1949)
Member of the U.S. Senate (1949-1960)
Vice-President (1961-1963)

POLITICAL PARTY
Democratic

INAUGURATED AS PRESIDENT
First term: November 22, 1962, aboard Air Force One,
Dallas, Texas
Second term: January 20, 1965, the Capitol,
Washington, D.C.

AGE AT INAUGURATION
55

DIED
San Antonio, Texas, January 22, 1973, age 64

RICHARD M. NIXON

THIRTY-SEVENTH PRESIDENT 1969–1974

Recalling Richard M. Nixon's sittings for this portrait late in 1968, Norman Rockwell claimed that Nixon was "the hardest man" he had ever had to paint. Rockwell also admitted that in painting the picture, he had consciously attempted to flatter his subject by, among other things, understating his prominent jowls and making his hair look thicker than it actually was. The problem, according to Rockwell, was that Nixon fell into the troublesome category of "almost good-looking," and apparently if Rockwell was going to go astray in his portrayal, he wanted to be sure that it was in a direction that would please his subject.

Richard Nixon was never directly involved in the host of illicit activities that became known as the Watergate scandals. But eventually investigations did indicate that he had taken part in the attempt to cover up this wrongdoing by members of his administration and his reelection committee. And that was enough to force his resignation. As he later said, "I let the American people down. And I have to carry that burden the rest of my life."

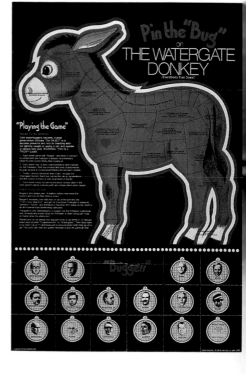

This photograph of Richard Nixon with his daughters, Tricia and Julie, and his wife, Pat, was taken during his tenure as vice-president to Dwight Eisenhower. Unlike most vice-presidents, Nixon played a vital role in the administration. He represented the president on diplomatic visits and took charge of the White House during Eisenhower's illnesses. This valuable experience laid the foundation for Nixon's later successes, especially in foreign affairs.

In late 1962, shortly after his defeat in the California gubernatorial election, Richard Nixon stood before an assemblage of news reporters and declared his intention to retire from politics. This announcement came as no surprise to his audience. In the House of Representatives, Nixon had not been known for warmth and easy likeability, and his sometimes unscrupulous efforts to undermine his political opponents had engendered considerable negative feeling. Nevertheless, during his eight years as Eisenhower's vice-president, he had performed admirably, both as acting president during Ike's several prolonged illnesses and as a representative of American interests abroad. But the failure of his own presidential candidacy in the election of 1960, followed by his unsuccessful bid for the California governorship, led many—including Nixon himself—to the conclusion that he had reached the end of the road politically.

Nixon's resolve to forswear politics did not, however, last long. Within a few years, he was once again taking an active role in promoting the Republican party. In doing so, he was also reemerging as a serious White House contender. On presidential election day in 1968, he claimed the very prize that had eluded him in 1960 and that in 1962 he had publicly indicated he would never seek again.

On the domestic front, Nixon's presidency was not particularly notable for lasting achievements. And although he ultimately kept his campaign promise to end the bitterly controversial war in Vietnam, many were highly critical of the slowness with which he moved toward that goal. But in other respects, Nixon's accomplishments were substantial. While the efforts of previous administrations to ease Cold War tensions with the communist world had never yielded many meaningful results, Nixon's attempts at peaceable rapprochement did. By the end of his first term, the United States was signing landmark agreements with the Soviet Union for mutual disarmament. More important, in partnership with Henry Kissinger, his foreign affairs adviser, Nixon finally opened the way for American recognition of communist China and a normalization of diplomatic relations with it.

Unfortunately, Nixon never had time to savor these accomplishments and to enjoy his growing reputation as an architect of a more constructive and considerably less threatening international order. During his 1972 campaign for a second term, his reelection committee engaged in a number of illegal activities, the most notable a conspiracy to wiretap Democratic party offices at the Watergate complex in Washington. As the probes into this election-year malfeasance progressed, it became clear that many of Nixon's closest advisers had been party to the wrongdoing. In the end many of them went to jail. Worse yet, it was eventually found that while not directly involved in the crimes that had initiated the Watergate investigations, Nixon had participated in attempts to cover up the scandal. As a result, by mid-1974 his credibility as a leader had totally evaporated, and the House of Representatives was preparing articles of impeachment accusing him of intentionally blocking the Watergate inquiries and of abusing his presidential powers. Rather than face a Senate trial on those charges, Nixon became the only president in history to resign from office.

BORN
Yorba Linda, California, January 9, 1913

ANCESTRY
English-Scottish-Irish-Welsh

WIFE
Thelma Catherine (Pat) Ryan
Born: Ely, Nevada
March 16, 1912

MARRIED
Riverside, California, June 21, 1940

CHILDREN
Patricia (1946-)
Julie (1948-)

EDUCATION
Whittier College, Whittier, California; B.A. (1934)
Duke University Law School, Durham, North Carolina;
LL.B. (1937)

RELIGION
Quaker

OCCUPATIONS
Lawyer, politician, and writer

MILITARY SERVICE
Rose from lieutenant, j.g. to lieutenant commander,
U.S. Navy (1942-1945)

PREPRESIDENTIAL OFFICES
Member of the House of Representatives (1947-1950)
Member of the U.S. Senate (1951-1953)
Vice-President (1953-1961)

POLITICAL PARTY
Republican

INAUGURATED AS PRESIDENT
First term: January 20, 1969, the Capitol, Washington, D.C.
Second term: January 20, 1973, the Capitol,
Washington, D.C.

AGE AT INAUGURATION
56

RESIGNED FROM PRESIDENCY
August 9, 1974

GERALD R. FORD

THIRTY-EIGHTH PRESIDENT   1974–1977

Despite its pin-striped formality, Gerald R. Ford's portrait has a congenial warmth that bespeaks one of the main strengths of his presidential leadership. As one observer put it shortly after he took office, Ford was, above all, "durable, dependable, and easy to live with," qualities which in themselves went a long way toward restoring credibility to the presidency following Richard Nixon's resignation.

Betty Ford, above, was an outspoken First Lady. Her public support of the Equal Rights Amendment and the legalization of abortion caused public controversy and embarrassment for her husband. She also spoke openly about her mastectomy, at a time when surgery for breast cancer was rarely publicized, and thus helped to inform and save the lives of countless American women. After Ford left office, she revealed that she was an alcoholic and also dependent on painkilling drugs. She went into treatment and recovered. To help others recover from chemical dependence she later helped found the Betty Ford Clinic, in Rancho Mirage, California.

Gerald Ford's pardoning of former President Richard Nixon for his role in the Watergate scandals was the most controversial act of his administration. Many were incensed that Nixon would never face trial for his alleged wrongdoings, and news of the pardon sent Ford's approval rating from 71 to 49 percent. To repair his damaged credibility, Ford decided to go before the House of Representatives' Judiciary Committee to explain the reasons for the pardon, and on October 17, 1974, he became the first president since Washington to testify before Congress. Pictured here on that occasion, Ford told the committee that, in his estimation, Nixon had already suffered sufficiently and that a trial of the former president would only distract the nation from dealing with its current problems. Although this was a reasonable explanation, Ford never fully recovered the popularity that the pardon had cost him.

The annals of presidential history include a number of stories about men who reached the White House through unusual and sometimes irregular sequences of events. There was, for example, John Quincy Adams, who had risen to the nation's highest office as a result of a deadlock in the electoral college and a political deal in the House of Representatives. And there was "dark horse" James K. Polk, who had emerged seemingly from nowhere to claim the presidency in 1844. But if historians were asked to name the president who came to office under the most unexpectedly bizarre set of circumstances, there could be only one answer—the thirty-eighth president of the United States, Gerald R. Ford.

Among the elements that make the story of Ford's rise to the presidency so singular was that Ford himself had never entertained the slightest desire for that office. He had been quite content with his position as a member of the House of Representatives, and after his election in 1965 as Republican minority leader, his only other ambition was to one day become Speaker of the House. In the face of his party's chronic inability to gain a majority in the House, however, the goal eluded him. By the early 1970s, with the prospects for a change in the political situation as remote as ever, Ford had almost decided that the time had come to retire from public life. But just as he was starting to consider leaving politics, an incredible chain of events began conspiring to prevent it.

On October 10, 1973, after pleading *nolo contendere* to a charge of tax evasion, Spiro T. Agnew, Richard Nixon's vice-president, resigned from office. Shortly thereafter, Nixon appointed Ford to the vice-presidency.

Then, just as the Senate began moving to confirm that appointment, Ford's political fortunes took yet another drastic turn; before he had fully settled into the vice-presidency it appeared that the mounting evidence of Nixon's involvement in the Watergate scandals might force the president to resign. Within another six months that possibility had become reality. On August 9, 1974, Ford became the only vice-president to succeed to the presidency because of the resignation of his predecessor.

In many respects, Ford's White House tenure was not a success. In his response to a sagging economy and high inflation, he proved largely ineffective, and in his efforts to devise solutions to the energy crisis caused by the great rise in oil prices, he often found himself blocked by a balking Congress. As far as many contemporary observers were concerned, however, Ford's greatest sin was his issuing of a blanket pardon to Nixon for any part he may have had in the Watergate scandals. The anger inspired by this act was enormous and, in its wake, Ford's approval rating plummeted sharply.

Nevertheless, Ford performed one service that on balance exceeded his shortcomings: Having come to office because of a scandal that reduced public faith in the presidency to its lowest point in modern memory, Ford met his responsibilities with an honesty and openness that to a great extent restored that lost credibility. In so doing, he proved that, even under the most trying circumstances, Americans' pride in the orderly workings of the constitutional system was not misplaced.

BORN
Omaha, Nebraska, July 14, 1913
(Original name: Leslie Lynch King, Jr.)

ANCESTRY
English

WIFE
Elizabeth Anne Bloomer
Born: Chicago, Illinios
April 8, 1918

MARRIED
Grand Rapids, Michigan, October 15, 1948

CHILDREN
Michael Gerald (1950-   )
John (Jack) Gardiner (1952-   )
Steven Meigs (1956-   )
Susan Elizabeth (1957-   )

EDUCATION
University of Michigan, Ann Arbor, Michigan; B.A. (1935)
Yale University Law School, New Haven, Connecticut;
LL.B. (1941)

RELIGION
Episcopalian

OCCUPATIONS
Football coach, lawyer, and politician

MILITARY SERVICE
Rose from ensign to lieutenant commander in U.S. Navy
(1942-1946)

PREPRESIDENTIAL OFFICES
Member of the U.S. House of Representatives (1949-1973)
House Minority Leader (1965-1973)
Vice-President (1973-1974)

POLITICAL PARTY
Republican

INAUGURATED AS PRESIDENT
August 9, 1974, East Room of the White House,
Washington, D.C.

AGE AT INAUGURATION
61

JIMMY CARTER

THIRTY-NINTH PRESIDENT   1977–1981

One of the trademarks of Jimmy Carter's political style was a sweater-and-blue-jeans informality that he quite consciously cultivated when reaching out to the electorate. But recording his likeness for posterity was quite another matter, and in this portrait, which Robert Templeton began at the White House in the late 1970s, the intention clearly was to invest Carter with a full measure of presidential dignity.

Rosalyn Carter was an activist First Lady in the tradition of Eleanor Roosevelt. During her first year in the White House, she made visits to eighteen countries, the most notable a mission to seven Latin American nations as an official spokesperson for the government. She was also generally credited with obtaining Congressional passage for the Mental Health Systems Act and lobbied actively for the Equal Rights Amendment. At times, Rosalyn Carter's role in affairs of state raised eyebrows, and after she attended a cabinet session in 1978, the press reported, "She's telling Jimmy what to do." "They obviously don't know Jimmy," she responded, and continued to attend cabinet meetings. This photograph of the Carters was taken by Ansel Adams.

The Iranian hostage crisis cost Jimmy Carter the support and faith of the American people and the 1980 presidential election. After a failed military rescue attempt, intense negotiations, and 444 days, the fifty-two hostages were finally freed on the last day of Carter's presidency.

84

Midway through Jimmy Carter's term as governor of Georgia, his mother teasingly asked him what he was going to do with himself when he was out of office. She was not expecting a serious answer. When Carter responded, "I'm going to run for President," she took it at first as a joke. But when she continued the joke by asking "President of what?" she realized from the thoughtful look on her son's face that upon leaving the governorship in 1975 he was indeed intent on running for president.

In achieving his White House ambitions, however, Carter had one seemingly insurmountable problem: Outside his own state, he was a political unknown. As he began campaigning for the Democratic presidential nomination early in 1976, one of the most frequently heard quips on the campaign trail was "Jimmy who?" But the question soon lost its cynical bite. By summer, armed with iron determination, a gleaming smile, and an appealingly down-to-earth manner, Carter had sewn up the nomination and, by year's end, was staking his claim to the presidency.

Carter owed his unexpected rise to the White House to a unique blend of populism and conservatism that promised both innovation and caution. He also owed it to his success in convincing voters that as a man who had not been jaded by many years as a Washington insider, he had a truer understanding of the country's current needs and a healthier perspective on just how those needs should be met.

But although Carter's party held majorities in both houses, his inability to deal effectively with Congress made it difficult for him to live up to the high expectations that his campaign rhetoric had engendered. Thus, his attempts to promote such measures as tax reform, national health insurance, and changes in the country's welfare system met, for the most part, with failure, and in implementing a national energy policy in response to the oil shortages of the 1970s, he proved at best only partially successful. Worse yet, he never succeeded in coming to grips with the inflationary spiral that had been plaguing the United States since the early 1970s. By early 1980, the nation's annual inflation rate was hovering around 16 percent.

Carter's administration did, however, manage to achieve some of its major objectives, among them the deregulation of the banking and air transportation industries and civil service reform. It was also largely due to Carter's intercession that Egypt and Israel finally negotiated an end to the state of war that had so long existed between them.

Unfortunately, these and other triumphs were not enough to counteract the widespread popular perception that Carter was not up to the job of leading the country. When, late in 1979, anti-American feeling in Iran climaxed with the taking of fifty-two hostages at the American embassy, and when Carter's efforts to free the hostages continually met with failure, that perception deepened even further. By mid-1980, his approval rating in the polls had reached an unprecedented low. Consequently, although the Democrats nominated him for a second term that year, enthusiasm for his candidacy even among many party faithful was far from wholehearted. Well before the election in November, it seemed clear to many that Carter's "political miracle" of 1976 would not repeat itself.

BORN
Plains, Georgia, October 1, 1924

ANCESTRY
English

WIFE
Eleanor Rosalynn Smith
Born: Plains, Georgia
August 18, 1927

MARRIED
Plains, Georgia, July 7, 1946

CHILDREN
John William (Jack) (1947-   )
James Earl (Chip) III (1952-   )
(Donnell) Jeffrey (1952-   )
Amy Lynn (1968-   )

EDUCATION
U.S. Naval Academy, Annapolis, Maryland; B.S. (1946)

RELIGION
Baptist

OCCUPATIONS
Naval officer, farmer, politician, writer, and philanthropist

MILITARY SERVICE
Rose from ensign to lieutenant commander, U.S. Navy (1946-1953)

PREPRESIDENTIAL OFFICES
Member of the Georgia State Senate (1963-1967)
Governor of Georgia (1971-1975)

POLITICAL PARTY
Democratic

INAUGURATED AS PRESIDENT
January 20, 1977, the Capitol, Washington, D.C.

AGE AT INAUGURATION
53

RONALD REAGAN

FORTIETH PRESIDENT   1981–1989

When Ronald Reagan became president in 1981, he was just short of his seventieth birthday, and some thought that he would not be up to the rigors of leading the country. Reagan did survive the demands of office, as well as an assassination attempt, and as this portrait, begun during his final months in the White House, indicates, the warm vitality that he had brought to the presidency was still very much intact as he prepared to leave it.

During her husband's term as president, reporters accused Nancy Reagan of being materialistic, cold, and calculating, and claimed she was the ultimate power behind the Reagan Administration. Near the end of his second term, there was great controversy and consternation when it was revealed that she consulted an astrologer to help guide her husband on matters of state policy. Michael K. Deaver, a close Reagan associate, defended Mrs. Reagan saying, "Those who clash with her will perpetuate the image of Nancy Reagan as the Invisible Hand, manipulating, ruthless in dealing not only with her husband's adversaries but with friends who let him down. Let the record show that she acted, when she acted, only to protect the President."

On March 30, 1981, as Ronald Reagan was leaving Washington's Hilton Hotel, where he had given a speech, John B. Hinckley, Jr., shot him, leaving fragments of a bullet lodged within three inches of the President's heart. Hinckley also shot several other men; the most seriously injured, Press Secretary James Brady, was shot in the head and suffered severe brain damage. Within a week the President was on his way to a full recovery and was joking about the incident with quips like, "Let's do this scene again, starting at the hotel" and to his wife, "Honey, I forgot to duck." It was later revealed that Hinckley shot the President to gain the attention of film actress Jodie Foster, who starred in the movie Taxi Driver, which dealt with a similar assassination scenario. It was a case of life imitating art and a macabre irony for a president who was once an actor.

In the 1940s, if anyone had claimed that a moderately successful screen actor named Ronald Reagan had the makings of a president, he would have been laughed at. By 1964, however, Reagan had become a spokesman for the Republican party's more conservative elements and, in the wake of his spellbinding televised speech that year in support of Republican White House hopeful Barry Goldwater, such an assertion no longer seemed so implausible. Although Reagan's masterful performance was not enough to make Goldwater president, it nevertheless demonstrated Reagan's own remarkable powers as a vote-getter. Almost overnight, a movement to put this one-time actor into public office was afoot and, two years later, he won election to the California governorship.

For Reagan's backers, this was only a beginning. No sooner had he settled into the governorship than his supporters were contemplating strategies for making him a presidential candidate. Initially these strategies proved unsuccessful; after he failed to win the Republican nomination in 1976, it almost seemed that Reagan's political career was at an end. In 1980, however, in the face of mounting distrust of the federal bureaucracy's capacity to deal with such problems as rampant inflation and a stagnating economy, Reagan's call for reducing the government's role in American life had great appeal to voters. Consequently, Reagan came to the Republican convention that year virtually unopposed for his party's presidential nomination. Six months later he was sworn in as president.

Reagan's disengaged White House style, which often manifested itself in a poor mastery of the details of his administration, did not augur well for a productive presidency. Yet Reagan had two strengths that more than made up for that detachment: He seemed to know what he wanted, and he had an almost magical ability to sell the American people on the rightness of his stated views. By the end of his two terms in office, his program to cut back on government regulation of the economy, substantially reduce taxes, decrease federal spending on social services, and drastically increase the country's military strength had been largely successful. His major failure was his disregard for achieving a balanced budget.

Falling short in that respect produced record annual deficits, which by the late 1980s was running into the trillions of dollars—a development that observers found increasingly worrisome. Also disturbing were indications that many of Reagan's advisers had used their positions for private gain and the revelations that his administration had conspired to circumvent a congressional ban on supplying military aid to anticommunist forces in politically troubled Nicaragua.

For most Americans, such things did not seem to matter much as they enjoyed the boom prosperity that resulted from Reagan's tax reforms and his loosening of federal controls over the economy. In addition, there was also a widely shared perception that Reagan's great military buildup in the name of curbing communist influence in the world might have played a part in the demise of the confrontational politics of the Cold War shortly after he left office. With a thriving economy and an easing of international tensions, the faults of Reagan's presidency paled and, when he left the White House in 1989, he commanded a popularity that few other outgoing presidents have enjoyed.

GEORGE BUSH

FORTY-FIRST PRESIDENT   1989–

This bust of George Bush dates from the early years of his vice-presidency. When Bush viewed the final bronze version, he warmly approved it. Nevertheless, he could not resist pretending indignation at the furrows that the sculptor had etched on his forehead.

George Bush's deep and avowed love for the family, and traditional values in general, was a major factor in his appeal to the American people. In the photograph above, taken when he was vice-president, he is surrounded by his family.

George Bush inherited a significantly different world from the one faced by his predecessor, Ronald Reagan. The Soviet Union was no longer the "evil empire." Through the changes initiated by Soviet President Mikhail Gorbachev, a new and friendlier relationship was established between the United States and the Soviet Union marking the end of the Cold War. Significant progress was made in arms control negotiations and treaties between the two countries, but more important were the changes in Eastern Europe. For the first time since World War II, the Soviets allowed Eastern Bloc countries the right of self-determination and permitted democratic elections. The most startling and dramatic events of 1990 were the destruction of the Berlin Wall and the reunification of Germany. Taken during Gorbachev's visit to Washington in the spring of 1990, this photograph shows the Soviet leader and Bush at the White House, signing a statement calling for further mutual arms reductions.

By the early 1960s, George Bush was presiding over a multimillion dollar oil business in Houston, Texas. Some have speculated that had he remained in that business, he might well have become a billionaire. But the prospect of building a modest fortune into an immense one did not hold much interest for this transplanted New Englander, and, in 1962, he turned his attention to making his way in politics. Four years later, after a stint as a Republican party county chairman and an unsuccessful bid for a seat in the United States Senate, he was elected to the House of Representatives where he eventually served two terms and soon earned a reputation as a comer in the Republican Party.

Bush's defeat in another try for the Senate in 1970 represented something of a setback in his political progress, but it was temporary. By the decade's end, his successes as ambassador to the United Nations, national chairman of the Republican party, envoy to China, and director of the Central Intelligence Agency began to make him look vaguely presidential.

In Bush's first attempt to gain his party's White House nomination in 1980, however, he ultimately lost to Ronald Reagan. Nevertheless, he emerged from the contest with a valuable consolation prize when Reagan tapped him to be his vice-presidential running mate. Given the immense popularity of Reagan's subsequent presidency, the worth of that prize turned out to be substantial indeed. In 1988, Bush's eight years of close identification with Reagan's successes became the springboard for his election to the presidency in his own right.

In future evaluations of Bush's administration, many historians will doubtless single out Bush's foreign policy as one of his most distinguished successes. In particular, they will note that it was Bush who put together and led the military coalition of world powers that opposed the occupation of Kuwait by Iraq's Saddam Hussein and ultimately drove the Iraqi armies from Kuwait. But it is less clear how his domestic policies will be viewed and whether his cautious line of action in such matters as urban crime, energy conservation, and the federal deficit will yield substantial results.

A personable and open man who seems entirely at ease with himself, Bush has been characterized as a leader unusually tolerant of disagreement who finds debate a useful tool in formulating his policies. Not an ideologue with a hard and fast agenda, he is, above all, a seeker of workable solutions to the problems at hand. When arriving at those solutions required sacrificing some of what he wanted for the sake of a larger goal, he frequently was willing to "split the difference."

It is also apparent that Bush likes being president. As one observer put it at the end of Bush's first year in office, "He works as hard at the job as Carter did, yet wears the office as lightly as Reagan."

BORN
Milton, Suffolk County, Massachusetts, June 12, 1924

ANCESTRY
English

WIFE
Barbara Pierce
Born: Bronx, New York
June 8, 1925

MARRIED
Rye, New York, January 6, 1945

CHILDREN
George Walker (1946-   )
Robin (1949-1953)
John Ellis (Jeb) (1953-   )
Neil Mallon (1955-   )
Marvin Pierce (1956-   )

EDUCATION
Yale University, New Haven, Connecticut; B.A. (1948)

RELIGION
Episcopalian

MILITARY SERVICE
Rose from ensign to lieutenant, j.g., U.S. Navy
(1942-1945)
Awarded Distinguished Flying Cross

OCCUPATIONS
Businessman and politician

PREPRESIDENTIAL OFFICES
Member of the U.S. House of Representatives (1967-1971)
U.S. Ambassador to the United Nations (1971-1973)
Chairman of the Republican National Committee
(1973-1974)
Chief of the U.S. Liaison Office in China (1974-1975)
Director of the Central Intelligence Agency (1976-1977)
Vice-President (1981-1989)

POLITICAL PARTY
Republican

INAUGURATED AS PRESIDENT
January 20, 1989, the Capitol, Washington, D.C.

AGE AT INAUGURATION
64

FACTS ABOUT THE PRESIDENTS

PRESIDENTS AND THEIR VICE-PRESIDENTS

GEORGE WASHINGTON: John Adams
JOHN ADAMS: Thomas Jefferson
THOMAS JEFFERSON: Aaron Burr, George Clinton
JAMES MADISON: George Clinton, Elbridge Gerry
JAMES MONROE: Daniel D. Tompkins
JOHN QUINCY ADAMS: John Calhoun
ANDREW JACKSON: John Calhoun, Martin Van Buren
MARTIN VAN BUREN: Richard M. Johnson
WILLIAM HENRY HARRISON: John Tyler
JOHN TYLER: None
JAMES K. POLK: George M. Dallas
ZACHARY TAYLOR: Millard Fillmore
MILLARD FILLMORE: None
FRANKLIN PIERCE: William R. King
JAMES BUCHANAN: John C. Breckinridge
ABRAHAM LINCOLN: Hannibal Hamlin, Andrew Johnson
ANDREW JOHNSON: None
ULYSSES S. GRANT: Schuyler Colfax, Henry Wilson
RUTHERFORD B. HAYES: William A. Wheeler
JAMES GARFIELD: Chester A. Arthur
CHESTER A. ARTHUR: None
GROVER CLEVELAND:
Thomas A. Hendricks, Adlai E. Stevenson
BENJAMIN HARRISON: Levi P. Morton
WILLIAM McKINLEY:
Garret A. Hobart, Theodore Roosevelt
THEODORE ROOSEVELT: Charles Warren Fairbanks
WILLIAM HOWARD TAFT: James S. Sherman
WOODROW WILSON: Thomas R. Marshall
WARREN G. HARDING: Calvin Coolidge
CALVIN COOLIDGE: Charles Gates Dawes
HERBERT HOOVER: Charles Curtis
FRANKLIN D. ROOSEVELT: John N. Garner,
Henry Agard Wallace, Harry S Truman
HARRY S TRUMAN: Alben W. Barkley
DWIGHT D. EISENHOWER: Richard M. Nixon
JOHN F. KENNEDY: Lyndon B. Johnson
LYNDON B. JOHNSON: Hubert Humphrey
RICHARD M. NIXON: Spiro Agnew, Gerald R. Ford
GERALD R. FORD: Nelson A. Rockefeller
JIMMY CARTER: Walter Mondale
RONALD REAGAN: George Bush
GEORGE BUSH: Dan Quayle

Presidents with Vice-President from a Different Party
JOHN ADAMS (Federalist):
Thomas Jefferson (Democratic-Republican)
ABRAHAM LINCOLN (Republican): Andrew Johnson
(Democratic)

President Who had Three Vice-Presidents
FRANKLIN D. ROOSEVELT (John N. Garner,
Henry Agard Wallace, Harry S Truman)

Vice-President Chosen by Senate
Richard M. Johnson (MARTIN VAN BUREN)

Vice-Presidents Who Resigned
John Calhoun (ANDREW JACKSON)
Spiro Agnew (RICHARD M. NIXON)

VITAL STATISTICS

Months of Birth

January: Millard Fillmore
William McKinley
Richard M. Nixon
Franklin D. Roosevelt
February:
William Henry Harrison
Abraham Lincoln
Ronald Reagan
George Washington
March: Grover Cleveland
Andrew Jackson
James Madison
John Tyler
April: James Buchanan
Ulysses S. Grant
Thomas Jefferson
James Monroe
May: John F. Kennedy
Harry S Truman
June: George Bush
July: John Quincy Adams

Calvin Coolidge
Gerald R. Ford
August: Benjamin Harrison
Herbert Hoover
Lyndon B. Johnson
September:
William Howard Taft
October: John Adams
Chester A. Arthur
Jimmy Carter
Dwight D. Eisenhower
Rutherford B. Hayes
Theodore Roosevelt
November: James Garfield
Warren G. Harding
Franklin Pierce
James K. Polk
Zachary Taylor
December: Andrew Johnson
Martin Van Buren
Woodrow Wilson

Height and Weight

Shortest
James Madison (5'4")

Tallest
Abraham Lincoln (6'4")

Six Feet and Over

Chester A. Arthur
James Buchanan
George Bush
Millard Fillmore
James Garfield
Warren G. Harding
Andrew Jackson
Thomas Jefferson

Andrew Johnson
John F. Kennedy
Abraham Lincoln
James Monroe
Ronald Reagan
Franklin D. Roosevelt
William Howard Taft
John Tyler

George Washington

Lightest
James Madison
(about 100 lbs.)

Heaviest
William Howard Taft
(332 lbs.)

Death

Age at Death
OLDEST: John Adams (90)
YOUNGEST: John F. Kennedy
(46)
**Died in Office
From Natural Causes**
Warren G. Harding
William Henry Harrison
Franklin D. Roosevelt
Zachary Taylor
**Died in Office
By Assassination**
James Garfield
John F. Kennedy
Abraham Lincoln
William McKinley

Died During First Term
James Garfield
Warren G. Harding
William Henry Harrison
John F. Kennedy
Zachary Taylor

Died During Second Term
Abraham Lincoln
William McKinley

Died During Fourth Term
Franklin D. Roosevelt

Died on the Fourth of July
John Adams
Thomas Jefferson
James Monroe

Served Shortest Term
William Henry Harrison (31 days)

Served Second Shortest Term
James Garfield (199 days)

Served Less Than One Term

Chester A. Arthur	William Henry Harrison
Millard Fillmore	Andrew Johnson
Gerald R. Ford	John F. Kennedy
James Garfield	Zachary Taylor
Warren G. Harding	John Tyler

Served One Term

John Adams	Rutherford B. Hayes
John Quincy Adams	Herbert Hoover
James Buchanan	Franklin Pierce
Jimmy Carter	James K. Polk
Benjamin Harrison	William Howard Taft
Martin Van Buren	

Served More Than One Term

Grover Cleveland	William McKinley
Calvin Coolidge	James Monroe
Dwight D. Eisenhower	Richard M. Nixon
Ulysses S. Grant	Ronald Reagan
Andrew Jackson	Franklin D. Roosevelt
Thomas Jefferson	Theodore Roosevelt
Lyndon B. Johnson	Harry S Truman
Abraham Lincoln	George Washington
James Madison	Woodrow Wilson

Elected to Second Terms

Grover Cleveland	William McKinley
Dwight D. Eisenhower	James Monroe
Ulysses S. Grant	Richard M. Nixon
Andrew Jackson	Ronald Reagan
Thomas Jefferson	Franklin D. Roosevelt
Abraham Lincoln	George Washington
James Madison	Woodrow Wilson

Served Two Terms

Grover Cleveland	James Madison
Dwight D. Eisenhower	James Monroe
Ulysses S. Grant	Ronald Reagan
Andrew Jackson	George Washington
Thomas Jefferson	Woodrow Wilson

Elected to Four Terms
Franklin D. Roosevelt

Served Non-Consecutive Terms
Grover Cleveland

Only President to Resign
Richard M. Nixon

Had Served as Vice-President

John Adams	Andrew Johnson
Chester A. Arthur	Lyndon B. Johnson
George Bush	Richard M. Nixon
Calvin Coolidge	Theodore Roosevelt
Millard Fillmore	Harry S Truman
Gerald R. Ford	John Tyler
Thomas Jefferson	Martin Van Buren

Served after Completion of Vice-Presidential Term

John Adams	Thomas Jefferson
George Bush	Richard M. Nixon
Martin Van Buren	

Only Vice-President to Succeed Because of Resignation of Predecessor
Gerald R. Ford

House of Representatives

John Adams	Andrew Johnson
James Buchanan	Lyndon B. Johnson
George Bush	John F. Kennedy
Millard Fillmore	Abraham Lincoln
Gerald R. Ford	James Madison
James Garfield	William McKinley
William Henry Harrison	Richard M. Nixon
Rutherford B. Hayes	Franklin Pierce
Andrew Jackson	James K. Polk
John Tyler	

Senate

John Quincy Adams	Lyndon B. Johnson
James Buchanan	John F. Kennedy
James Garfield (did not serve)	James Monroe
Warren G. Harding	Richard M. Nixon
Benjamin Harrison	Franklin Pierce
William Henry Harrison	Harry S Truman
Andrew Jackson	John Tyler
Andrew Johnson	Martin Van Buren

Department of State

John Adams	William Henry Harrison
John Quincy Adams	Thomas Jefferson
James Buchanan	James Monroe
George Bush	Martin Van Buren

Department of the Treasury

Collector of Port of New York: Chester A. Arthur
Internal Revenue Service: William Howard Taft

Post Office Department

Postmasters: Abraham Lincoln, Harry S Truman

Governors

Governor-General of the Philippines
William Howard Taft

Military Governors
Andrew Jackson
Andrew Johnson

Provisional Governor of Cuba
William Howard Taft

Territorial Governor of Indiana
William Henry Harrison

State Governors
CALIFORNIA: Ronald Reagan
GEORGIA: Jimmy Carter
MASSACHUSETTS: Calvin Coolidge
NEW JERSEY: Woodrow Wilson
NEW YORK: Grover Cleveland
Franklin D. Roosevelt
Theodore Roosevelt
Martin Van Buren
OHIO: Rutherford B. Hayes
William McKinley
TENNESSEE: Andrew Johnson
James K. Polk
VIRGINIA: Thomas Jefferson
James Monroe
John Tyler

EDUCATION

Attended College But Did Not Graduate	Did Not Attend College	Graduated from College	
Warren G. Harding	Grover Cleveland	John Adams	Rutherford B. Hayes
William Henry Harrison	Millard Fillmore	John Quincy Adams	Herbert Hoover
Thomas Jefferson	Andrew Jackson	Chester A. Arthur	Lyndon B. Johnson
William McKinley	Andrew Johnson	James Buchanan	John F. Kennedy
James Monroe	Abraham Lincoln	George Bush	James Madison
John Tyler	Zachary Taylor	Jimmy Carter	Richard M. Nixon
	Harry S Truman	Calvin Coolidge	Franklin Pierce
	Martin Van Buren	Dwight D. Eisenhower	James K. Polk
	George Washington	Gerald R. Ford	Ronald Reagan
		James Garfield	Franklin D. Roosevelt
		Ulysses S. Grant	Theodore Roosevelt
		Benjamin Harrison	William Howard Taft
		Woodrow Wilson	

Colleges Attended

Allegheny College
William McKinley

Amherst College
Calvin Coolidge

Bowdoin College
Franklin Pierce

College of William and Mary
Thomas Jefferson
James Monroe
John Tyler

Dickinson College
James Buchanan

Eureka College
Ronald Reagan

Hampden-Sydney College
William Henry Harrison

Harvard University
John Adams
John Quincy Adams
John F. Kennedy
Franklin D. Roosevelt
Theodore Roosevelt

Johns Hopkins University
Woodrow Wilson

Kenyon College
Rutherford B. Hayes

Miami Univeristy (Ohio)
Benjamin Harrison

Ohio Central College
Warren G. Harding

Princeton University
John F. Kennedy
James Madison
Woodrow Wilson

Southwest Texas Teachers College
Lyndon B. Johnson

Stanford University
Herbert Hoover

Union College
Chester A. Arthur

U.S. Military Academy (West Point)
Dwight D. Eisenhower
Ulysses S. Grant

U.S. Naval Academy (Annapolis)
Jimmy Carter

University of Michigan
Gerald R. Ford

University of North Carolina
James K. Polk

Whittier College
Richard M. Nixon

Williams College
James Garfield

Yale University
George Bush
William Howard Taft

Graduate School

Received Ph.D.
Woodrow Wilson

Studied Medicine
William Henry Harrison

Attended Law School
Lyndon B. Johnson
William McKinley
Franklin D. Roosevelt
Theodore Roosevelt
Harry S Truman
Woodrow Wilson

Graduated Law School
Gerald R. Ford
Rutherford B. Hayes
Richard M. Nixon
William Howard Taft

Law Schools Attended
Albany Law School
William McKinley

Cincinnati Law School
William Howard Taft

Columbia University Law School
Franklin D. Roosevelt
Theodore Roosevelt

Duke University Law School
Richard M. Nixon

Georgetown University Law School
Lyndon B. Johnson

Harvard Law School
Rutherford B. Hayes

Kansas City School of Law
Harry S Truman

University of Virginia Law School
Woodrow Wilson

Yale University Law School
Gerald R. Ford

Studied Law
John Adams
John Quincy Adams
Chester A. Arthur
James Buchanan
Grover Cleveland
Calvin Coolidge
Millard Fillmore
Gerald R. Ford
James Garfield
Benjamin Harrison
Rutherford B. Hayes
Andrew Jackson
Thomas Jefferson
Lyndon B. Johnson
Abraham Lincoln
William McKinley
James Monroe
Richard M. Nixon
Franklin Pierce
James K. Polk
Franklin D. Roosevelt
Theodore Roosevelt
William Howard Taft
Harry S Truman
John Tyler
Martin Van Buren
Woodrow Wilson

ASSASSINATIONS

Presidents Assassinated
James Garfield
John F. Kennedy
Abraham Lincoln
William McKinley

Attempted Assassinations
Jimmy Carter
Gerald R. Ford
Andrew Jackson
Ronald Reagan
Harry S Truman

AUTHORS

Wrote Books

John Adams	Benjamin Harrison	Richard M. Nixon
John Quincy Adams	Herbert Hoover	Ronald Reagan
James Buchanan	Thomas Jefferson	Franklin D. Roosevelt
Jimmy Carter	Lyndon B. Johnson	Theodore Roosevelt
Grover Cleveland	John F. Kennedy	William Howard Taft
Calvin Coolidge	James Madison	Harry S Truman
Dwight D. Eisenhower	William McKinley	George Washington
Gerald R. Ford	James Monroe	Woodrow Wilson

Poet
John Quincy Adams

MILITARY SERVICE

U.S. Navy
World War II
George Bush
Gerald R. Ford
Lyndon B. Johnson
John F. Kennedy
Richard M. Nixon
Korean War
Jimmy Carter
U.S. Army
Revolution
Andrew Jackson
James Monroe
George Washington
War of 1812
William Henry Harrison
Andrew Jackson
John Tyler

Black Hawk War
Abraham Lincoln
Zachary Taylor
Mexican War
Ulysses S. Grant
Franklin Pierce
Zachary Taylor
Civil War
Chester A. Arthur
James Garfield
Ulysses S. Grant
Benjamin Harrison
Rutherford B. Hayes
Andrew Johnson
William McKinley

Spanish American War
Theodore Roosevelt

World War I
Dwight D. Eisenhower
Harry S Truman
World War II
Dwight D. Eisenhower
Ronald Reagan

Generals
Chester A. Arthur
Dwight D. Eisenhower
James Garfield
Ulysses S. Grant
Benjamin Harrison
William Henry Harrison
Rutherford B. Hayes
Andrew Jackson
Andrew Johnson
Franklin Pierce

Zachary Taylor
George Washington

Professional Soldiers
Dwight D. Eisenhower
Ulysses S. Grant
William Henry Harrison
Zachary Taylor

Wounded or Injured in Action
Rutherford B. Hayes
Andrew Jackson
John F. Kennedy
James Monroe

Prisoner of War
Andrew Jackson

OCCUPATIONS OF THE PRESIDENTS

Actor
Ronald Reagan

Businessman
George Bush

Farmers and Planters
John Adams
Jimmy Carter
Thomas Jefferson
Zachary Taylor
George Washington

Haberdasher
Harry S Truman

Lawyers
John Adams
John Quincy Adams
Chester A. Arthur

James Buchanan
Grover Cleveland
Calvin Coolidge
Millard Fillmore
Gerald R. Ford
James Garfield
Benjamin Harrison
Rutherford B. Hayes
Andrew Jackson
Thomas Jefferson
Abraham Lincoln
William McKinley
James Monroe
Richard M. Nixon
Franklin Pierce
James K. Polk
Franklin D. Roosevelt
William Howard Taft

John Tyler
Martin Van Buren
Woodrow Wilson

Law Professor
William Howard Taft

Newspapermen
Warren G. Harding
John F. Kennedy
William Howard Taft

Presidents of Universities
Dwight D. Eisenhower
(Columbia University)
Woodrow Wilson
(Princeton University)

Publisher
Warren G. Harding

Schoolteachers
John Adams
Chester A. Arthur
Millard Fillmore
James Garfield
Warren G. Harding
Lyndon B. Johnson
William McKinley

Surveyors
John Adams
Abraham Lincoln
George Washington

ACKNOWLEDGMENTS

The Presidents was conceived, developed and produced by Gramercy Books and the Book Development Division, Smithsonian Institution Press.

Gramercy Books: Glorya Hale, Editorial Director; Frank Finamore, Assistant Editor; Bill Akunevicz, Jr. and Jean Krulis, Designers; Debra Borg, Picture Researcher; Ellen Reed, Production Supervisor.

Book Development Division, Smithsonian Institution Press: Caroline Newman, Executive Editor; Paula Ballo Dailey, Picture Editor; Heidi Lumberg, Assistant Editor.

Special thanks to Keith Melder and the Division of Political History, National Museum of American History; Beverly Cox, Claire Kelly, Pam Kirschner, and Frances Stevenson, National Portrait Gallery; and the Office of Printing and Photographic Services.

PICTURE CREDITS

Abbreviations are used to identify Smithsonian Institution collections:

NPG	National Portrait Gallery
NMAH	National Museum of American History
ANR	Division of Agriculture and Natural Resources
DPH	Division of Political History
NPC	National Philatelic Collection
DT	Division of Textiles

Legend: **T** Top; **C** Center; **B** Bottom; **L** Left; **R** Right

Jacket: detail, Gilbert Stuart (1755-1828), oil on canvas, 1796 (48 x 37 in.), owned jointly by the National Portrait Gallery and the Boston Museum of Fine Arts.

Back jacket and half title page: courtesy of the White House.

Title page: NMAH/DPH; **pages 4-9:** NMAH/DPH.

p. **10TR** Gilbert Stuart (1755-1828), oil on canvas, 1796 (48 x 37 in.), owned jointly by the National Portrait Gallery and the Boston Museum of Fine Arts; **10TL** NMAH/NPC; **10BL** Edward Savage (1761-1817), and David Edwin (1776-1841), after Edward Savage, stipple engraving, 1798 (24½ x 18 7/16 in.), NPG.

p. **12TL** John Trumbull (1750-1831), oil on canvas, 1793 (25⅝ x 21½ in.), NPG; **12C** NMAH/DPH; **12BL** NMAH/DPH.

p. **14TR** Gilbert Stuart (1755-1828), oil on panel, 1805 (26⅛ x 21 in.), NPG, owned jointly with Monticello, gift of the Regents of the Smithsonian Institution, the Trustees of the Thomas Jefferson Memorial Foundation, and the Enid and Crosby Kemper Foundation; **14TL** NMAH/DPH; **14BL** NMAH/DPH.

p. **16TR** Chester Harding (1792-1866), oil on canvas, 1829/30 (30 x 25 in.), NPG; **16L** William S. Elwell (1810-1881), oil on canvas, 1848 (30 x 25 in.), NPG; **16BR** Bernard Francis Hoppner Meyer (1811-?), after John Wesley Jarvis, stipple engraving, 1830-1840 (8¼ x 6⅞ in.) NPG.

p. **18TL** John Vanderlyn (1775-1852), oil on canvas, 1816 (26½ x 22⅜ in.), NPG; **18TR** NMAH/DPH; **18BR** NMAH/DPH.

p. **20TR** George Caleb Bingham (1811-1879), oil on canvas, *c.*1844 (37⅛ x 32 3/16 in.), NPG; **20BL** Kelloggs and Comstock lithography company (active 1848-1850), hand-colored lithograph, 1848, (11⅞ x 8 9/16 in.), NPG; **20BR** NMAH/DPH.

p. **22TR** Ralph E. W. Earl (1788?-1837), oil on canvas, not dated (25½ x 30 in.), NPG; **22C** NMAH/DPH; **22BR** Francisco Scacki (active 1815), etching, engraving, aquatint, and soft ground, 1815 (16 x 23 13/16 in.), NPG.

p. **24TL** Matthew Brady (1829-1896), daguerreotype, *c.*1856 (5½ x 4 5/16 in.), NPG; **24TR** NMAH/DPH; **24BR** A.A. Hoffay (active 1830s), John Dorival, lithographer, lithograph, 1818 (19⅛ in. x 14⅝ in.), NPG.

p. **25B** NMAH/DPH.

p. **26TR** Albert Gallatin Hoit (1809-1856), oil on canvas, 1840 (30 x 25 in.), NPG; **26TL** NMAH/DPH; **26BL** Henry R. Robinson (active *c.* 1831-*c.*1841), hand-colored lithograph, 1841 (9 x 13 3/16 in.), NPG.

p. **28TL** George P.A. Healy (1813-1894), oil on canvas, 1859 (36⅛ x 29⅛ in.), NPG, transfer from the National Museum of American Art; **28C** James Barton Longacre (1794-1869), sepia watercolor on artist board, 1830 (8⅞ x 6⅜ in.), NPG; **28BL** NMAH/DPH, from original in Valentine Museum, Richmond, VA.

p. **30TL** Miner Kellogg (1814-1889), oil on canvas, 1848 (26½ x 22 in.), NPG, on long-term loan from the Cincinnati Art Museum; **30TR** Nathaniel Currier (1813-1888), hand-colored lithograph, 1844 (12 11/16 x 9⅜ in.), NPG; **30BL** NMAH/DPH.

p. **31B** NMAH/DPH.

p. **32TR** attributed to James Reid Lambdin (1807-1889), oil on canvas, 1848 (30¼ x 24¾ in.), gift of Barry Bingham, Sr., NPG; **32TL** NMAH/DPH; **32BL** William Garl Brown, Jr. (1823-1894), oil on canvas, 1847 (30 x 36 in.), NPG.

p. **33B** NMAH/DPH.

p. **34TL** unidentified artist, oil on canvas, *c.*1840 (30 x 25 in.), NPG; **34TR** NMAH/DPH; **34BL** Robert Whitechurch (1814-*c.*1880), after Peter Frederick Rothermel, after daguerreotypes, engraving, 1855 (27 x 34 3/16 in.), NPG, gift of Mrs. Richard K. Doud.

p. **36TR** George P.A. Healy (1813-1894), oil on canvas, 1853 (30 x 25¼ in.), NPG, transfer from the National Gallery of Art, gift of Andrew W. Mellon; **36TL** NMAH/DPH; **36BL** Eliphalet M. Brown, Jr. (1816-1866), after Peter Bernard William Heine Sarony lithography company, lithograph with printed and hand-tinted color, 1855 (20 9/16 x 32½ in.), NPG, gift of August Belmont IV.

p. **38TL** George P.A. Healy (1813-1894), oil on canvas, 1859 (62 x 47 in.), NPG, transfer from the National Gallery of Art, gift of Andrew W. Mellon; **38TR** NMAH/DPH; **38BL** Thomas Murphy Johnston (1834-1859), probably after photograph by James Wallace Black, after daguerreotype attributed to Martin M. Lawrence, lithograph, 1859 (12⅛ x 10⅝ in.), NPG; **38BR** unidentified photographer, ambrotype, 1856 (4 3/16 x 3⅜ in.), NPG, gift of an anonymous donor.

p. **39B** NMAH/DPH.

p. **40TR** George P.A. Healy (1813-1894), oil on canvas, 1887 (74 x 54 in.), NPG, transfer from the National Gallery of Art, gift of Andrew W. Mellon; **40TL** NMAH/DPH; **40BR** NMAH/DPH; **40BL** Alexander Hay Ritchie (1822-1895), after Francis Bicknell Carpenter, engraving, 1866 (20⅞ x 32⅜ in.), NPG, gift of Mrs. Chester E. King.

p. **42TR** Washington Bogart Cooper (1802-1889), oil on canvas, *c.*1865, (36¼ x 29¼ in.), NPG; **42TL** Thomas Nast (1840-1902), pastel cartoon, irregular, not dated (51½ x 40½ in.), NPG; **42BL** Mathew Brady (1823-1896), or his studio, photograph, albumen silver print, 1868, (6¾ x 9 in.), NPG.

p. **44TL** Thomas LeClear (1822-1885), oil on canvas, *c.*1880 (53¾ x 31¾ in.), NPG, transfer from the National Museum of American Art, gift of Mrs. Ulysses S. Grant, Jr.; **44TR** Pach Brothers studio, active since 1867, photograph, albumen silver print, *c.*1883,

(7¹/₁₆ x 9⁵/₁₆ in.), NPG; **44BR** Ole Peter Hansen Balling (1823-1906), oil on canvas, 1865 (120 x 192 in.), NPG, gift of Mrs. Harry Newton Blue.

p. 45B NMAH/DPH.

p. 46TL Olin Levi Warner (1844-1896), plaster, 1876 (10⅞ in.), NPG, gift of Mrs. Carlyle Jones; **46TR** Thomas Hicks (1823-1890), oil on canvas, c.1870 (53 x 32¾ in.), NPG; **46BL** NMAH/DPH.

p. 48TL Ole Peter Hansen Balling (1893-1906), oil on canvas, 1881 (24 x 20 in.), NPG, gift of International Business Machine Corporation; **48TR** NMAH/DPH; **48BR** Major & Knapp lithography company (active 1864-1880s), lithograph, c.1881 (13¼ x 19⅜ in.), NPG.

p. 50TR Ole Peter Hansen Balling (1893-1906), oil on canvas, 1881 (24⅛ x 20⅛ in.), NPG, gift of Mrs. Harry Newton Blue; **50TL** NMAH/DPH; **50BL** Buek and Lindner lithography company (active 1880s), after photographs, Root and Tinker, publishers, chromolithograph, 1882 (18 x 24 in.), NPG.

p. 52TL Anders Zorn (1860-1920), oil on canvas, 1899 (48 x 36 in.), NPG, gift of Reverend Thomas G. Cleveland; **52C** NMAH/DPH; **52BL** NMAH/DPH.

p. 53B NMAH/DPH.

p. 54TR Eastman Johnson (1824-1906), charcoal and chalk on paper, c.1895 (18 x 12 in.), NPG; **54TL** Harris and Ewing studio, (active 1905-1977), photograph, gelatin silver print, c.1908 (14¾ x 11¼ in.), NPG, gift of Aileen Conkey; **54BR** NMAH/DPH.

p. 56TL August Benziger (1867-1955), oil on canvas, 1897 (58¾ x 39 in.), NPG, gift of Miss Marieli Benziger; **56TR** NMAH/DPH; **56B** Pach Brothers studio (active since 1867), photograph, albumen silver print, 1901 (9¾ x 12½ in.), NPG.

p. 57B NMAH/DPH.

p. 58TL Sally James Farnham (1876-1943), bronze relief, 1906 (20⅝ x 20⅝ in.), NPG; **58C** Underwood and Underwood, active 1882-c.1950, photograph, brown-toned gelatin silver print, 1906 (10 x 8 in.), NPG, gift of Joanna Sturm; **58BL** Pach Brothers studio, active since 1867, photograph, gelatin silver print, 1903 (14¹⁵/₁₆ x 3⁵/₁₆ in.), NPG, gift of Joanna Sturm.

p. 60TR Robert Lee MacCameron (1866-1912), oil on canvas, 1909 (39½ x 31⅞ in.), NPG, gift of Robert F. MacCameron and his sister, Marguerite MacCameron; **60TL** NMAH/DPH; **60B** William Dinwiddie (1867-1934), photograph, platinum print, 1905 (2¹¹/₁₆ x 6¹/₁₆ in.), NPG, gift of Joanna Sturm.

p. 62TR Edmund Tarbell (1862-1938), oil on canvas, 1921 (46 x 36¼ in.), NPG, transfer from the National Museum of American Art, gift of the City of New York through the National Art Committee, 1923; **62C** John Cristen Johanson (1876-1964), oil on canvas, 1919 (69½ x 64 in.), NPG, transfer from the National Museum of American Art, gift of an anonymous donor through Mrs. Elizabeth Rogerson, 1926. **62BR** American Lithographic Company (active c.1918), color lithographic poster, 1918 (30 x 20 in.), NPG, gift of PosterAmerica.

p. 64TL Margaret Lindsay Williams (1887-1960), oil on canvas, c. 1923 (53½ x 39¼ in.), NPG; **64C** Harris and Ewing studio (active 1905-1977), photograph, gelatin silver print, 1921 (9 x 6¹/₁₆ in.), NPG, gift of Aileen Conkey; **64BL** NMAH/DPH.

p. 65B NMAH/DPH.

p. 66TL Joseph Burgess (1891-1961) after an original by Ercole Cartotto (1899-1946), oil on canvas, 1956 (56½ x 38¼ in.), NPG, gift of the fraternity of Phi Gamma Delta; **66C** unidentified photographer, photograph, gelatin silver print, 1927 (9⅛ x 7¼ in.), NPG; **66BL** Keystone View company (active 1892-c. 1970), photograph, gelatin silver print, 1924 (3¹/₁₆ x 6 in.), NPG.

p. 68TL Douglas Chandor (1897-1953), oil on canvas, 1931 (45 x 38 in.), NPG; **68TR** NMAH/DPH; **68BR** NMAH/ANR.

p. 69B NMAH/DPH.

p. 70TR Douglas Chandor (1897-1953), oil on canvas, 1945 (53¾ x 45¾ in.), NPG; **70C** Trude Fleischmann (born 1895), photograph, gelatin silver print, 1944 (12¼ x 10¼ in.), NPG; **70BR** NMAH/DPH.

p. 71B NMAH/DPH.

p. 72TL Greta Kempton (born 1903), oil on canvas, begun 1948 and completed 1970 (39 x 30 in.), NPG, gift of members of Truman's administration; **72TR** Ben Shahn (1898-1969), color lithograph, 1948 (43 x 27½ in.), NPG; **72BR** Augustus Vincent Tack (1870-1949), oil on canvas, 1949, (95½ x 97 in.), NPG, gift of the Phillips Collection.

p. 73B NMAH/DPH.

p. 74TR Thomas E. Stephens (1886-1966), oil on canvas, 1947 (46 x 35 in.), NPG, transfer from the National Gallery of Art, gift of Ailsa Mellon Bruce; **74TL** courtesy of the United States Postal Service; **74BR** NMAH/DPH; **74BL** NMAH/DPH.

p. 76TR William Draper (born 1912), oil on canvas, 1966, from a life sketch of 1962 (40 x 32 in.), NPG; **76C** AP/Wide World Photos; **76BR** NMAH/DPH.

p. 79B NMAH/DPH.

p. 78TR Peter Hurd (1904-1984), tempera on panel, 1967 (48 x 38 in.), NPG, gift of the artist; **78TL** NMAH/DPH; **78BR** NMAH/DPH; **78BL** Garry Winogrand (1928-1984), photograph, gelatin silver print, 1969 (12¼ x 18½ in.), NPG.

p. 78B NMAH/DPH.

p. 80TR Norman Rockwell (1894-1978), oil on canvas, 1968 (18¼ x 26¼ in.), NPG, gift of the Nixon Foundation; **80CL** NMAH/DPH; **80CR** NMAH/DPH; **80BL** NMAH/DPH.

p. 81B NMAH/DPH.

p. 82TR Everett R. Kinstler (born 1926), oil on canvas, 1987 (44 x 34 in.), NPG, gift of the Gerald R. Ford Foundation; **82TL** AP/Wide World Photos; **82BL** AP/Wide World Photos.

p. 83B NMAH/DPH.

p. 84TR Robert Templeton (born 1929), oil on canvas, 1980 (92 x 56 in.), NPG, partial gift of the 1977 Inaugural Committee; **84BL** Ansel Adams (1902-1984), photograph, Polacolor print, 1980, (4½ x 3⁷/₁₆ in.), NPG, gift of Mr. and Mrs. James Earl Carter, Jr.; **84BR** NMAH/DPH.

p. 85 NMAH/DPH.

p. 86TR Henry Casselli, Jr. (born 1946), oil on canvas, 1989 (50 x 32 in.), NPG, gift of friends of President and Mrs. Reagan; **86TL** AP/Wide World Photos; **86BL** AP/Wide World Photos.

p. 87B NMAH/DPH.

p. 88TL Marc Mellon (born 1951), bronze, 1982 (24¾ inches), National Portrait Gallery, Smithsonian Institution, gift of Vincent and Sheila Downey Melzac. NPG; **88TR** AP/Wide World Photos; **88BR** AP/Wide World Photos.